RIGHT HERE,
RIGHT NOW

RIGHT HERE, RIGHT NOW

Spiritual Exercises for
Busy Christians

Christopher Carstens, Ph.D.
Rev. William P. Mahedy

A Ballantine/Epiphany Book
Ballantine Books • New York

A Ballantine/Epiphany Book

Library of Congress Cataloging in Publication Data

Carstens, Christopher, 1948-
  Right here, right now

  1. Spiritual life. I. Mahedy, William P., 1936-
II. Title.
BV4501.2.C327 1985   248.3   84-24238
ISBN 0-345-31801-3

Manufactured in the United States of America

Text design by Holly Johnson

First Edition: September 1985

10 9 8 7 6 5 4 3 2 1

This book is devoted to those closest to us: Linda, Jessica, and Adrian Carstens; and Carol, Michael, and Marie Mahedy.

Contents

Acknowledgments

The authors are grateful to Michelle Rapkin of Ballantine Books for her interest in *Right Here, Right Now* and for her suggestions on how to improve the manuscript. We are grateful also to Julie Garriott for her careful editing. Our thanks to Sandra Dijkstra, our literary agent, for her help and encouragement at every step along the way. Finally, we are especially grateful to Linda Carstens, whose editing, proofreading, and insightful comments greatly improved this book.

An Invitation

Right Here, Right Now was written for a special group of people—busy Christians. You are the people who work all day teaching school, and then drive home quickly in order to spend time with your own children—and after their bedtime, you start making calls for the church newcomers committee. And you are the parents who drive car pools and teach church school classes and go from door to door for the mission fund. And you are the people who own small businesses and bring work home every night, and wish you had more time for prayer. And some of you are members of the clergy, so caught up in meeting the needs of your congregation that you find yourself wondering whether any energy will be left for your own spiritual life.

You are committed Christians. Protestant or Catholic, you have chosen to follow Jesus. You may need inspiration and renewal from time to time, but you do not need to be convinced of the basic tenets of the Christian life. You believe that Jesus has called you to live in faith and that your lives are better because you have heeded that call. You may not be perfect Christians, but you have clearly decided to walk on the Christian path.

You are not satisfied to be passive observers of life,

and so you have immersed yourselves in life's activities and responsibilities. You have jobs or families, or jobs *and* families, and find yourselves running from one place to another, one task to another, a great deal of the time.

Finally, you sense an inadequacy in your spiritual lives. It can seem impossible to be active and prayerful at the same time, and as committed Christians you feel dissatisfied when the only time you can find for prayer and reflection is in church on Sunday morning. You know that your relationship with God demands more than the hour or so that you put into Sunday worship.

Right Here, Right Now is a book grown out of our own wrestling with the problem of developing time for prayer while leading busy lives. The ensuing brief spiritual exercises—some of them taking literally one minute's attention—are our attempt to make that problem smaller. Ours is not a "self-help" book, because we believe that Christians do not help themselves to spiritual renewal, but recognize that God helps them to it. Instead, we offer a guidebook to help the busy Christian become more open to the working of the Spirit in his or her everyday life. God is always available to us, but we are often not available to Him.

Right Here, Right Now is about stepping back from the frantic pace of our lives and making room for God to enter. It is not a theological treatise; we have nothing new to say about the nature of God. Our focus is more on the nature of people and how we can endeavor to turn ourselves more constantly to God. This is also not a book of learned essays on prayer. Our shared notion of prayer is a simple one: We believe that if we open ourselves to God's presence, He will work in us and through us. We have many suggestions for finding ways to open the doors of the heart to the Spirit, but very little to say about just how the Spirit will choose to work in a given life. Finally, this book is not a study of the spiritual truths passed down by great Christian writers. Readers seeking the wisdom of the long line of western Christian mystics are urged to read the primary sources, of which a brief annotated bibliography is provided at the end of the book.

Right Here, Right Now is designed for practicality. We intend it to be useful to people seeking new ways to pray, and new ways to find time for prayer. The book speaks to individual worshipers, and to pastors helping the members of their congregations find a more fruitful spiritual orientation for their lives. Finally, *Right Here, Right Now* is likely to find a home with groups of Christians who read, study, and pray together.

We invite you to participate actively in this book. There are many places where we will ask you to stop reading and more directly engage yourself in learning. It is our hope, and our prayer, that you will find *Right Here, Right Now* helpful as you seek your own closer relationship with God.

1 · Busy Christians

If you read this book, there is, willy-nilly, another book you will never read. Go to Spain, and you may not have time to go to England. Do the laundry, and you'll have given up a chance to clean out the garage. Spend more time with your children tomorrow, and there will be less of it available to devote to your spouse. Every day, the limits on your time force you to make choices. You cannot do everything.

Time is money, we sigh—you can only spend it once. And that bit of wistful wisdom seems true enough; but spent *time* can't be begged, borrowed, or stolen (or even earned) back. When it's gone, it's truly gone.

Some people seem to manage time surprisingly well, squeezing more activity into an hour than the rest of us can get into half a day. Nonetheless, even the best of time managers eventually run out of time. Time is the final limit on our earthly lives.

How do you spend your time? Most of us never sit down and take a careful look at the way we choose to use this precious gift.

At this point we introduce your first right-here, right-now pencil-and-paper exercise. It is best to do each exercise immediately, as you come upon it in the book, *before* reading on. These exercises are designed to help you learn about yourself and to make it easier to master new approaches to prayer. Of course, you may decide to simply read through the exercises without doing them. You will reach the last page of the book much more quickly that way, and could no doubt find other important uses for the time thus gained. On the other hand, you stand to gain a lot of territory in your quest for a closer relationship with God if you involve yourself in this part of the discovery.

Pencil-and-Paper Exercise 1: How You Spend Your Time

Let's look at how you are currently spending your time. Take a sheet of paper and draw a large circle on it. You'll make a "pie-chart" showing what percentage of your time you devote to each major activity of your life. This sort of chart is probably familiar to you: Governmental agencies and charitable institutions love to use them to illustrate how carefully they have spent our money!

Draw slices of the pie to show how many hours of your average twenty-four-hour day are devoted to each of your important (or unimportant but time-consuming) activities. Most of us spend eight hours asleep each day. Many people spend nine hours a day, five days each week, at a job and doing work-related activities such as commuting. You may spend one hour *per day* watching television, and so on. Don't worry about the fact that each day is different, or that you may often be doing two things at once. Approximations are good enough at this point.

If you are an employed woman with children, your chart for a work day might look something like this:

Don't read on until you've drawn your own pie chart.

2

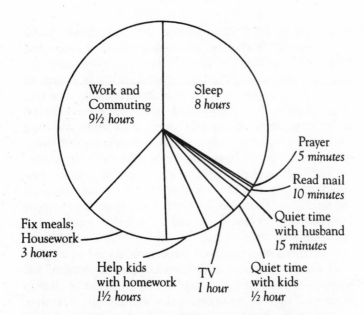

Work and
Commuting
9½ hours

Sleep
8 hours

Prayer
5 minutes

Read mail
10 minutes

Quiet time
with husband
15 minutes

Fix meals;
Housework
3 hours

Help kids
with homework
1½ hours

TV
1 hour

Quiet time
with kids
½ hour

Having completed your pie chart, take a careful look at it. How much of your time is regularly devoted to prayer or other activities designed expressly to enhance your relationship with God? In this estimate, do not include church-related pursuits such as organizing parish bazaars or typing the congregation's newsletter. While these are important things to do, they are not necessarily spiritual activities.

If you're like most of us, you will find that the slice of your time given to prayer is very thin indeed. One of the authors recently had a conversation with a woman who was very active in the life of her church, taking part in committees within the congregation and playing an important role in church-sponsored social action campaigns in her community. Indeed, she was a model church member, the type any clergyman or clergywoman would be thrilled to find in the congregation. At one point in the conversation she poignantly said that she would like to take a year off from church activity—in order to get her prayer life together.

If you talk with people about the reality of prayer in their lives, you will often hear comments like the one this woman made. We are all caught up in a day-to-day stream of activity, doing things that need to be done. Because we have to make decisions about how we use our time, and because we all have responsibilities and obligations, the time left over to devote to prayer can be meager. Just about anybody you know will confess to being snared in the same trap, the same "busyness." The question for most busy people who take their religion seriously seems to be, "How do I balance all this?" It takes a great deal of time to maintain a marriage, be a reasonably good parent, succeed on the job, and snatch an occasional moment for relaxation. How can you find God in the midst of all this activity? There is the occasional nagging realization that one hour in church on Sunday is only a nod in God's direction. It would be nice to do more—but there just is not enough time.

Life can begin to feel like a treadmill. Economic survival demands long hours on the job, even when both spouses are employed. Putting food on the table, paying the bills, and keeping the mortgage or rent current are major concerns for most people. In addition, the house has to be cleaned and laundry must be done. There are letters to be answered. The kids need to be driven to baseball practice; their homework must be supervised. With recent changes in family patterns, husbands are doing more of the household chores than ever before—but still, few people retire at night feeling no household task has been left undone. There is also a lot of competition for whatever time is left over after the basic tasks have been completed. The PTA calls you to be on the board, the church committee on new members wants you to attend a meeting, the choir wants you to sing tenor, and you might want to take an evening class to improve your chances of getting a promotion. Finally, if you are a single parent, you are faced with doubled overloads on the time and energy circuits.

Pencil-and-Paper Exercise 2: Your Job List

For this exercise, define a job as any activity you are obliged to do. The obligation can be formal, as with paid employment, or personal, as with your obligation to ensure that your children get their homework done at night. If somebody you care about would be surprised or angry if you did not complete a certain task, then it probably is *your* job. For example, if your spouse usually does dinner dishes but you do them now and then, it is not *your* job. On the other hand, if you have agreed to do the laundry and nobody has clean clothes unless you get them washed, laundry is your job. If you are secretary of the committee on Laotian refugees, doing the minutes each month is your job.

Jobs include only those things you are obligated to do. Things you do of your own volition, just because you enjoy them or find them personally rewarding, are not jobs.

Take a piece of paper and list your jobs—the things that you *have to get done.* Plan to spend about five minutes writing this list.

Don't read on until you have completed your job list.

Looking at your job list is likely to discourage the idea of becoming more involved in prayer—there's no time left. Yet most busy Christians realize that we must somehow make more room for God in our lives. Sunday worship isn't enough because it often seems to have little impact on the rest of the week.

5

Prayer doesn't become integrated into your daily routine because the time has already been filled up with things you *must* do. Faced with the conflicting demands on your time, you may pray only rarely outside Sunday services. Saint Paul urged us to pray without ceasing, but the only thing that continues ceaselessly in most of our lives is growth of the job list.

Prayer is not a job. Nobody gets angry at you if you don't get around to morning prayers. The demands of daily living are loud and insistent, while the call of God is quiet and easily ignored in the urgency of getting things done. You may hear that call at odd and unpredictable moments between your jobs or in the course of doing them, but most of us are soon distracted again and the opportunity is lost.

There are ways out of this predicament. You could take a pencil and draw a line through those jobs you don't want to do anymore and could legitimately give up. This would probably be a good idea—a lot of us clutter up our lives with jobs that we do not really need to do—but odds are that you will still be busy. Our jobs that are most time-consuming will not be so easily given up.

Another solution is to be done with the entire list and retire to a religious order. This can be an excellent solution, but to the majority of us it is neither available nor appealing—especially when we consider that people in religious life probably have about as many jobs to do as the rest of humanity. Celibate clergy may not have to meet the demands of family life, but parishioners can fill up all a priest's available time with their own needs. The job of the Christian minister has a way of expanding to take up almost the full twenty-four-hour day.

We propose another solution: If you cannot remake your job list so that you have big blocks of time for prayer, then you can make small spaces for prayer in the midst of all of your jobs. Our basic tactic is the one-minute spiritual

6

exercise, which can actually be completed in sixty seconds, in the middle of a busy day.

In the Forty-sixth Psalm there is a very clear statement of God's gentle, undemanding yet persistent call to prayer:

"Pause a while and know that I am God."
Psalms 46:10 *

You need to stop *doing things* and remember that you lead your busy life in the presence of God. You need to briefly halt the endless parade of busy thoughts and turn your mind to Him. You *can* learn to live as a prayerful person in the busy world. The goal of the one-minute spiritual exercises is to draw upon an ongoing relationship with God to sanctify your busy comings and goings.

Each of our one-minute spiritual exercises is based upon traditional forms of Christian spirituality. If you have read any of the writings of the great Christian mystical thinkers, you are likely to have found that the how-to-do-it parts were very hard to find—and that, once located, they turned out to demand large amounts of time.

We have attempted to adapt the spiritual exercises presented by these great thinkers so as to make prayer more accessible in all our lives. We describe the one-minute exercises in detail, and offer suggestions for fitting them into one's daily routine.

Prayer is not a panacea; prayer is not a self-improvement device designed to guarantee wealth, professional success, or a better sex life. Prayer is a way of developing a relationship with God. Our focus is not on perfecting people, but rather on helping imperfect people come into more meaningful contact with God, day by day.

*Excerpt(s) from *The Jerusalem Bible,* copyright © 1966 by Darton, Longman & Todd, Ltd. and Doubleday & Company, Inc. Reprinted by permission of the publisher.

2 · The One-Minute Way

How long is a minute? It's sixty seconds, one sixtieth of an hour, one 1,440th of a day, one 37 millionth of a seventy-year life span. But how long is a minute *really*? Minutes "feel" longer or shorter, depending on what you are doing. It's often hard to pin down what makes a minute pass by quickly or slowly, but we all know that there are very real differences in how quickly time seems to pass.

Pencil-and-Paper Exercise 3: How Long Is a Minute?

This exercise requires a timepiece with a second hand or digital readout of seconds, as well as pencil and paper. You will need the watch or clock for more of the exercises in this and other chapters, so you might want to keep it handy as you read.

Begin by timing a minute. In this part of the exercise, just sit and watch the second hand as it moves. Stop reading *now*, and look at your watch or clock while one minute passes—and as you do, observe what's happening in your mind.

Don't read on until you have timed one minute.

Now that you've timed the minute, think about what your mind was doing during those sixty seconds. Did the time seem long or short? Did your mind wander to different things? What things?

Get your paper and pencil ready. Write down the thoughts that came to you during the sixty seconds you spent watching the clock. However, rather than taking as much time as you might like, time yourself: Let yourself write for only *one minute*. Keep an eye on the second hand, and stop writing as soon as sixty seconds have passed. (This may feel a bit artificial, but it is part of the exercise.)

Don't read on until you've written for one minute about your reflections.

Did you find that the two timed minutes felt unequal in duration? It's quite likely that the first minute seemed rather long—there was not enough going on to fill your mind. The sense of how long the second minute lasted probably depended upon how much you had to write about. If you wrote "Nothing much happened" and then felt finished, the second minute may have seemed as empty— and as long—as the first. On the other hand, if you felt filled with ideas that you wanted to express on paper while you also tried to keep track of the passing seconds, the second minute may have felt uncomfortably brief: Time was rushing by faster than you wanted it to.

It turns out that our perception of time is quite elastic— so much so that it seems time itself is elastic. This is important to remember, especially as you go into the one-minute spiritual exercises. If you think about one minute as a hopelessly brief interval, the idea of one-minute prayer seems silly, almost irreligious. But if you realize that a minute can be a relatively long, potentially productive time, it becomes sensible and exciting to do spiritual exercises within that kind of time limit.

In terms of actually "getting things done," there may not be a great deal that you can accomplish in one isolated minute. You cannot build a birdhouse or play a game of cards or renew your prayer life. Probably none of your "jobs" can be completed in one minute. However, a lot of our important thinking and problem solving seems to get done during, or as a result of, short intervals of concentration. Reflect on the way you solve your major problems or make your big decisions. You may spend several days or weeks making a serious decision such as whether or not to sell your house or go back to college. It can take a long time to make some decisions, especially the painful or risky ones.

If you have a month to make an important decision, you certainly do not spend all of the 40,320 minutes in those four weeks thinking about the one problem. Even in considering a job change or a proposal of marriage, you are likely to concentrate on the decision for only a minute or so at a time—several times each day. The more important the decision is, the more often your thoughts will return to it briefly, as you consider the issues over and over and over. The rest of your time you spend thinking about other things, and doing jobs requiring a level of concentration that keeps you from thinking about anything other than the task at hand.

Pencil-and-Paper Exercise 4: Thinking About a Problem

Take out a sheet of paper. At the top of the paper, write down a question that states one of the major problems in your life needing resolution *right now*. It might be, "Should I sell my car and buy a moped?" "Should I give up my job as chair of the committee on tithing?" Or it might be something completely different. The important thing is to select a problem that is a major issue for you right now. As soon as you've written the question, look at your clock or watch. Then think for one minute about the possible solutions to your problem. Try hard not to think about anything else during this minute.

Don't read on until you've spent sixty seconds considering solutions to your problem.

What went on in your mind during the timed minute of problem solving? Many people find it surprisingly difficult to concentrate for a full minute on a single issue. Our minds wander; we jump from idea to idea. Some people can maintain their focus longer than others—it's a matter of temperament, or sometimes just experience—but very few of us can concentrate on a single thing for long periods of time without some sort of assistance. Many of us make up for this limitation by using aids for concentration: We write down our ideas, or we take a warm bath. Others improve concentration by doing a job that occupies the hands but leaves the mind mostly free, like knitting or painting a fence. Don't be at all surprised if you find it hard just to sit down and think about a problem, even a very important problem, for more than a minute.

During the days or weeks that you are involved in the process of solving a difficult problem or making an important decision, your mind is never idle on the issue, even when you aren't actively concentrating on it. The human mind is quite capable of doing several things at one time, and recent research goes so far as to suggest that your mind goes on with its problem solving even during sleep! In one fascinating study, a young man was a subject both in sleep research and in psychoanalysis. His dreams were carefully recorded in the sleep lab; his problem-solving efforts were noted by his analyst. Later comparison of the two records clearly demonstrated that his dreams developed out of and continued the problem-solving efforts he was making in his psychotherapy.

The process of working a problem through to its reso-

11

lution is carried on both day and night: quietly in the "back rooms" of the mind, and actively, in brief but intensive periods of conscious consideration. Occasionally the question is decided almost immediately, by some brilliant flash of insight. Most of the time, however, sound decisions or solutions to problems emerge from long stretches of intermittent consideration—with the active part done about one minute at a time.

Pencil-and-Paper Exercise 5: Watching the Mind Work on Two Things at Once

It's quite possible that you have been engaged in this process of thinking about two things at once while reading the last page or so. The previous exercise focused your mind on an important problem or decision in your life. The one minute of reflection probably "got the wheels turning" on that particular issue, and you probably continued to think about your question as you read the several paragraphs immediately following the exercise. Take some time (no need to watch the clock on this one) to reflect on ways that your problem-solving activity continued while you read, and on other occasions during which you have worked on mental problem solving while keeping busy at other things. Write down your reflections.

Don't read on until you have reflected for some time on how your mind can do two things at once, and have written down your reflections.

Except in entertaining idle thoughts, once you begin thinking about something, you can't just "turn it off" at will. How many times have you found that your mind was simply too full of thoughts to let you sleep? If our minds

12

are drawn to an issue, the process of problem solving continues long after we have turned our conscious attention to something else.

The same mental abilities that enable you to solve problems while doing other things can be an important force in the renewal of your prayer life. You may feel constrained to answer Saint Paul's admonition with "I *can't* pray without ceasing—I have too many other things to do." But we believe that one's mental activity can become prayerful, directed to God and His place in one's life.

Focus the mind intentionally on God for one minute at a time, several times a day, and your thinking will become better attuned to His presence and informed by it. This makes new openings for God to enter your life and work through you: Prayer is the work of God through man.

As you turn your mind to Him in brief moments of reflection, His work can begin to be more truly manifested in your life. As you continue seeking answers to your important questions, God's presence will be a force in your thinking.

One minute is not enough—not all by itself. Lives are rarely changed in a minute, but prayer can transform a life *one minute at a time.*

People who wish to become more prayerful have long relied on spiritual exercises. A spiritual exercise is a tool of prayer, designed to lead the mind into new ways of looking at things, into renewed awareness of God's work in our lives. Spiritual exercises interrupt the ordinary stream of thought and make a quiet place for God's entry. However, most traditional Christian spiritual exercises were developed in monastic communities and require blocks of time that most of us do not have available.

The following chapters introduce a series of spiritual exercises, most of which are designed to be completed in a minute snatched from the middle of a busy day. You can do them in the supermarket, on the freeway, while making breakfast, or during Sunday worship. The busy Christian cannot leave "the World" in order to find God: He has given us too many things to do exactly where we are.

3 · Finding Time for Prayer: Your Personal Rule of Life

The hardest thing about prayer can be finding time for it; something always comes up. Good intentions are lovely, but unless they lead to new behaviors, they're not particularly useful. The cliché says, "You always have time to do the things you really want to do." That cliché is a lie. It is often very hard to find time to do the things you really want to do, even when they're very important. Willpower alone is not enough. Given the complex and competing demands on your time, consistently coming up with the time to do anything new is difficult, and can seem impossible.

From time to time, those of us who are not athletes decide that we need to "shape up." The result of this good intention is usually two or three weeks of jogging, weight lifting, or walking two miles a day. Unfortunately, before long, old habits and the demands of daily living usually crowd out exercise. The same thing can easily happen to new attempts at prayer. Over the long run you won't gain much from two weeks of regular prayer, any more than you'd gain long-term fitness from two weeks spent swimming laps in a pool.

Pencil-and-Paper Exercise 6: Good Intentions Gone Astray

It's hard to work *anything* new into your daily schedule. Whether the plan is to start exercising more often or to read ten pages of the Bible every night, enthusiasm has a way of getting lost. It's much easier to keep doing what you've always been doing than it is to make a change in your behavior.

Make a list of activities you recall having begun (with the intention of repeating them routinely), but dropped after a few days or weeks. These should be *new positive activities* you tried to start, rather than *old bad habits* you tried to give up. For example, include an attempt to walk more, but not a plan to give up chocolate. Other possibilities might include a resolution to write daily "to do" lists, a plan to answer all letters the day you get them, or a firm decision to play baseball with your son every night this summer, "no matter what." Spend about three or four minutes listing the good habits you tried to establish but quickly gave up.

Make your list now.

When you have finished your first list, add a list (on the same sheet of paper) that shows your *successful* attempts at instituting positive new activities. These do not have to be things you continued to do forever once you started them; there are always changes in our lives. However, list new activities you kept up for several months or longer. Perhaps you were able to set up a schedule by which you regularly visited a relative in a nursing home; or you may have been successful in finding time to practice your piano every day. List some successful changes.

Make your second list now.

When you've finished both lists, compare them, one to the other. Does a long look reveal consistent differences between the two lists—between those activities that became regular parts of your life and those that did not? Spend a few minutes looking at your lists. If you note any patterns, write them down.

Don't read on until you have completed this exercise.

It's easy to start a new program of behavior, and hard to keep it up when the first rush of enthusiasm is gone. Before you begin the one-minute spiritual exercises, think about how to build time for prayer into your life: Prayer is a long-term spiritual journey. The traveller who begins a journey without looking at a road map and planning the trip often ends up going in circles (or nowhere at all). One of the differences between your two lists may have been that you maintained new activities when you had made a plan for working them into your daily life.

Many people continue active prayer for years and years. But many more seem to become excited about prayer after a particularly good sermon or mission, only to burn out on the prayer effort soon after beginning it. The difference seems to be that for those who continue praying, prayer has become as consistent a part of daily life as brushing their teeth. Talk with these successful "long-term prayers" and you'll find that most of the have made a decision that prayer will happen at certain times or places day after day. They no longer need to decide, "Shall I pray today?" The pattern has been established, and the *occasion* of prayer—though not, of course, its content—has become almost automatic.

The members of religious communities, monks and nuns, are often successful in maintaining consistent prayer; and although most of us do not choose their path, we can learn much from the pattern of their lives. All on their own, monks and nuns would probably have just as much trouble keeping at their prayers as do the rest of us. However, they live under a Rule of Life that keeps them involved with prayer. The rule states when, where, and how prayer is to occur. Each community has its own rule, growing out of its particular history and personality, but all provide for a regular, daily pattern of prayer. Most communities, following the example of Saint Benedict and his monks, come together two or more times each day to sing psalms, read the Scriptures, and pray together in an ancient service called the Divine Office, or the Hours. The Office sets out a steady rhythm of prayer tied to the liturgical year. In all communities, much time is also set aside for silent prayer and solitary reading. The entire day of the contemplative is structured to provide the most possible opportunities for prayer. Work—be it teaching, farming, or baking—is seen as an outgrowth and extension of the life of prayer. The monk or nun need not decide whether or not to pray; the decision has already been made.

The Rule of Life is a tool for maintaining prayer. It helps one begin praying in the morning, when prayer often feels difficult, and supports the effort of prayer during the inevitable periods of lost enthusiasm. The rule is what translates today's spiritual high into a lifelong journey.

Reflective Exercise 1: The Parable of the Sower

Pencil and paper are not needed for this exercise. The reflection—an introduction to one-minute prayer—is to last one minute. You will need to time your reflection with a watch or clock.

Consider the following selection from the twentieth chapter of Matthew.

'Now the kingdom of heaven is like a landowner going out at daybreak to hire workers for his vineyard. He made an agreement with the workers for one denarius a day, and sent them to his vineyard. Going out at about the third hour he saw others standing idle in the market place and said to them, "You go to my vineyard too and I will give you a fair wage." So they went. At about the sixth hour and again at about the ninth hour, he went out and did the same. Then at about the eleventh hour he went out and found more men standing round, and he said to them, "Why have you been standing here idle all day?" "Because no one has hired us," they answered. He said to them, "You go into my vineyard too." In the evening, the owner of the vineyard said to his bailiff "Call the workers and pay them their wages, starting with the last arrivals and ending with the first." So those who were hired at about the eleventh hour came forward and received one denarius each. When the first came, they expected to get more, but they too received one denarius each. They took it, but grumbled at the landowner. "The men who came last," they said, "have done only one hour, and you have treated them the same as us, though we have done a heavy day's work in all the heat." He answered one of them and said, "My friend, I am not being unjust to you; did we not agree on one denarius? Take your earnings and go. I choose to pay the last-comer as much as I pay you. Have I no right to do what I like with my own? Why be envious because I am generous?" Thus the last will be first, and the first, last.'

Matthew 20:1–16

Think about this passage for sixty seconds. What is the Gospel saying to you about time and the spiritual journey? Odd though it may feel, time your reflection. Do not stop before sixty seconds are up, nor continue longer.

Don't read on until you have finished your sixty-second reflection.

People who maintain the effort of prayer over months and years have almost always developed a plan that they follow every day. They can be said to live under a personal rule of life. Usually the personal rule is developed through a trial-and-error process.

Few of us ever sit down and think through a plan for prayer—but perhaps more of us should. Careful planning can lead to the development of a much more helpful personal rule. A well-designed rule will help you consistently find time to pray and will help you be persistent in your prayer. The difference between those who successfully maintain long-term prayer and those who don't may lie less in the quality of the individual than in the quality of the rule he or she has devised.

The best way to make prayer a regular part of your life is to develop a personal rule of life linking prayer with the existing patterns of your day. It may seem that your day has very few patterns to which anything can be linked, yet most of us actually lead more or less tightly structured lives. We do many things in the same way almost every day. There are many "automatic" behaviors in each of our lives—things we do without being reminded to do them, or without even thinking much about them.

Here are some examples of things that happen "automatically" in the lives of many people. Some of them are almost certainly familiar to you.

- Have a cup of coffee
- Wake the children
- Let the dog out
- Shave
- Brush your hair
- Put on makeup
- Turn on the radio or TV
- Eat breakfast
- Read the front page of the paper
- Lock the door
- Start the car to drive to work
- Make a telephone call
- Open your mail

- Take a coffee break
- Eat lunch
- Fill in a daily time report, or punch a clock
- Eat dinner
- Write a letter
- Read a book
- Do the newspaper crossword puzzle
- Brush your teeth
- Put on your nightclothes

Enough! It's clear that in your life there are repeated activities. You do some of them once a day at about the same time every day, others over and over during the day.

Pencil-and-Paper Exercise 7: List Your Own Automatic Behaviors

Make a list of your automatic behaviors, moving through the day in sequence. Think about the patterns of your day—the activities you do morning, noon, and night. This is not a test of memory skills, so don't be too concerned with setting things down in perfect order.

Don't read on until you have listed your automatic behaviors.

The key to developing a successful personal rule of life is to link prayer to activities that already happen "by themselves."

Select one or two of your automatic behaviors and then commit yourself to carrying out your brief spiritual exercise every time you are *about* to assume the automatic behavior. It's crucial that you do the spiritual exercise *first*; then the automatic mechanism will remind you that it's time to pray. If you decide to pray for a minute *before* you open the mail, be absolutely willing to let the mail go unopened until you spend your minute in prayer. Your desire to see what's in that interesting envelope from New York will prod you into prayer much more effectively and consistently than your good intentions ever could.

The pattern just won't work if you try it the other way around. If you try to pray *after* the automatic act, the rule will break down: There will always be something to distract you. Decide to pray *after* you start the car, and instead of praying, you will quickly find yourself thinking about where you are going in your car. Start your spiritual exercise *after* your first cup of coffee, and you will end up moving on to your next automatic behavior without a pause for prayer. The linking works only when the new behavior is inserted *before* the automatic behavior.

The one-minute exercises are designed to open your conscious mind briefly to God's presence. They are most effective if they are scattered throughout your day. If you drive a lot, one minute of prayer each time you are about to start your car will mean that several minutes of prayer are slated into your day. Similarly, a sixty-second prayer before each cup of coffee can bring you into contact with God over and over during times when you would otherwise be absorbed in your work or in other activities. The mental work of prayer begun in these captured minutes will continue long after you have ended the exercise and returned to your regular activities.

When you first set up your personal rule, it is likely to feel quite artificial. However, as time goes on, prayer will become a more natural part of your life. For example, one of the authors established a very strong pattern of morning prayer by committing himself to a period of prayer before reading the sports page. Prayer came before the baseball scores—an excellent moral lesson as well! Eventually prayer in the morning took on a very special place in the rhythm of the author's day. However, it was the personal rule, linking prayer with the happily entrenched habit of looking up the box scores, that made morning prayer a regular event. It was the continuing commitment to that linking that led to persistence of prayer in the face of the inevitable distractions. The children always need to be fed breakfast, and the lawn often needs watering—it would be easy to do those things *instead* of praying. However, no matter how busy the morning is, the sports page is *never* forgotten—and it is never read until *after* prayers. If there's not enough time for prayer, there is not enough time for the sports page either. Somehow, the time is usually found.

Deciding to pray more often and deciding to pray for one minute before morning coffee are both good intentions. However, one is merely a general attitude; the other is a specific plan. To translate your good intentions into a workable personal rule of life, take a series of steps.

Pencil-and-Paper Exercise 8: Writing Your Personal Rule of Life

- Review your list of automatic behaviors. This list is the raw material for your personal rule. Select one or two of these events that happen several times each day. Circle them on your list.
- Try to imagine what would really happen if you prayed for one minute before the behavior or behaviors you have chosen. Would the prayer interfere with your life in some predictable way? This is a time to be very realistic with yourself: If prayer before a particular activity would be consistently inconvenient, you'll probably soon give up trying to pray. If on reflection you find that this is likely to happen to you, given the specific behavior you've chosen, select a different one. For example, if you drive for a car pool, it would be hard to take a serene minute to pray before turning on your car; you're aware your riders would not appreciate the wait should your timing be off. Think through such realities in advance, before you go further with writing your personal rule.

- Write down your personal rule of life. It might look something like this:

  I, Marie, will pray for one minute before I drink my orange juice in the morning and before I eat any snacks during the day.

  or

  I, David, will pray for one minute before I turn on the radio to listen to the news.

  or

  I, Frank, will pray for one minute before I play a tape in my car, unless I am travelling with someone else. I will also pray for one minute before I comb my hair.

- You have written your personal rule of life; now sign it! Something in the making of a commitment to a written, signed rule is very motivating, even if you never show the document to anyone else.

Don't read on until you have written and signed your personal rule of life.

At this point you have a personal rule, but no one-minute prayer exercises for making the most of it. A number of different exercises are presented in the next three chapters. Chapters 7 through 9 contain exercises that require longer periods of time, and for those we'll suggest special modifications of the personal rule to accommodate them. You are likely to change your personal rule many times. Certain times for prayer will work out well, others will turn out to be surprisingly inconvenient or even impossible. Feel free to modify the rule to meet reality—it is, after all, your own.

The traditions of the church offer a wide and varied spiritual banquet. Select from the exercises presented those that appeal to you most. You cannot do them all at the

24

same time. So much of life would be spent in prayer that there wouldn't be any left over for lunch, much less a busy work schedule. After you have tried the different exercises in the book, pick one or two and do them on a sustained basis. Later, you might want to add another, or substitute a new exercise for one that you have been doing for a while.

The personal rule of life is not magic; it's a tool. But it is a very useful tool. By writing your own rule and living by it, you can bring prayer into your life on a consistent, fulfilling basis. Without such a rule the answer to the question, "When shall I pray?" is very often, "Someday, when I have enough time." Once you have a personal rule the answer becomes, "Right here, right now."

4 · Practicing the Presence of God: Simple One-Minute Meditations

At one time or another, almost everyone has played the mental game based on the idea that one has been given something of great value, but with distinct limits placed on its use: What would you do if someone handed you ten thousand dollars to spend *today*? If you learned you had one more year to live? Where would you go if you could visit any one country in the world? Helen Keller, born without sight or hearing, once wrote a moving essay about what she would do if she could see for three days.

What would you do if you had one minute to pray?

Time for prayer can certainly be precious, but one minute (unless it's our last) doesn't seem like enough time to get very excited about. Yet one minute of prayer—one minute of contact with our Lord—can work a powerful change in mental direction.

One of the crucial events in the history of the church took place in one minute of contact with God. Saul was busy rounding up members of a small Jewish cult, the Christians. He was knocked to the ground by his encounter with Christ—"Saul, Saul, why are you persecuting me?" (Acts 9:4)—and was struck blind in that moment, his entire vision of the world forever altered. He emerged from the encounter, sight restored, as Paul, one of the most important leaders in the foundation of the church. Your minutes of prayer may not be quite that dramatic. But if you open yourself to God, He will change your life. Like Saul, you will be unable to go on living as you did before; and things will certainly look different to you after the experience.

The main goal of the one-minute exercises is to help you *stop* whatever you are doing, saying, or thinking and make an opening for God to enter. When you are doing no more than maintaining the rapid pace of your daily activities, that "just keeping up" can be so consuming that prayer seems impossible. However, once you decide to stop, to "waste" a minute with God, your pattern of "hurry, hurry, hurry" is broken. The stream of one automatic behavior flowing into the next is briefly stemmed—and prayer becomes possible.

The idea of spending one minute in prayer, no more and no less, is meant to be taken quite literally. Time yourself with a watch or clock, because it's very easy to misjudge the passage of time. Timing yourself is the only way to make sure that the exercises actually last one minute—and this is not a trivial matter. If you consistently take longer periods of time for your prayers or reflections, on the presumption that longer is better, you'll eventually find it easy to say to yourself, "I really don't have time to do this right now, I'll do it *next time.*" This sort of thinking is quite likely to lead to the breakdown of your personal rule. Stopping before your sixty seconds are up can have equally bad effects.

You can carry out the exercise without really disrupting the stream of your automatic behaviors. One minute can seem like a long time when you are in a hurry. The full minute is needed to step back from the flow of activity and get another perspective on what you are doing. So whenever your rule tells you it is time to pray, look at a watch or clock and time your sixty-second retreat.

One-Minute Spiritual Exercise 1: Stop, Relax a Minute with God

As with the pencil-and-paper exercises, it is a good idea to do each one-minute spiritual exercise when you first read about it. This will let you get a sense of how the exercises work, and how they "feel." The step-by-step practice will also help you develop a sense of how long a minute lasts, and will aid you in acquiring the skill of timing yourself as you pray.

Your first one-minute spiritual exercise is the simplest, but potentially one of the most profound. Brother Lawrence of the Resurrection, a seventeenth-century French Carmelite monk, developed a rich spiritual life based on what he referred to as "the Practice of the Presence of God." Quite simply, the practice consists of remembering that God is indeed with you in the present moment. This one-minute exercise, drawn from Brother Lawrence's practice, consists of relaxing, clearing your mind, and turning your attention to the fact that God is present with you, wherever you are, whatever you are doing.

To do the exercise, sit as comfortably as you can, letting your legs and arms relax. Place one hand on your abdomen, with your thumb about at the level of your navel and the hand resting below it, against your abdomen. You will notice that your hand rises and falls as you breathe, rising with each inhalation and falling with each exhalation.

Look at a watch or clock, and then breathe slowly, your hand rising and falling, for one minute. The first time you do the exercise, do not attempt anything more than timing out sixty seconds of calm, regular breathing. Perhaps you will notice that you become more relaxed as you breathe. Just allow that to happen; don't worry about whether or not you reach some "deep" state of relaxation. This is, after all, only a one-minute exercise.

Having done it once, try it again. This second time, however, attempt to focus on the presence of God as you relax. Survey your surroundings as you breathe, and know that Christ is present with you in this very place; you do not need to look anywhere else to find him. Spend a minute breathing, your hand slowly rising and falling, letting the awareness of God's presence develop.

Don't read on until you have relaxed a minute with God.

Once you feel comfortable relaxing for a minute with God, you can move on to other, more complex one-minute spiritual exercises. However, please remember that a simple openness to the loving presence of God in this moment of your life is both your initial spiritual exercise in this book *and* the final goal of all other spiritual exercises a Christian might undertake in a lifetime.

Each of the remaining one-minute exercises here and in the next two chapters begins with a brief inventory of the present moment. Since you'll be doing these exercises in different settings, it's important to begin each one by taking stock of your situation at the moment of prayer. Where are you? What have you just been doing, and what will you be doing immediately after the exercise? What are you thinking about or feeling emotionally in the present moment? You will begin each of the remaining one-minute spiritual exercises with a few seconds spent reviewing your present situation and sharing it with God. Your inventory might run something like this:

"Right now I'm sitting in my bedroom, reading a book about prayer, Lord. I feel excited about what might come of it, but unsure, too. Also, it's late at night, and I'm tired."

"Lord, I'm in the middle of a miserable traffic jam, and what I want to do most is get home. I'd like to turn on the radio, but I agreed to pray for a minute first, so here goes...."

or

"I feel great, God. I've just been with some friends and I'm walking home with my head full of thoughts about their lives."

In turning your attention to your current situation and offering that awareness to God, you step back from what you are doing. The very act of noticing your present state and reflecting upon it grants you a sense of distance. The stream of automatic behavior has been diverted from its usual course.

One-Minute Spiritual Exercise 2: A Conversation with God

Begin with your inventory of the present moment: Where are you, what are you doing, thinking, and feeling? Then simply talk with God for one minute about whatever is on your mind. In your review of the present moment, the most prominent feeling may be anger. Spend sixty seconds sharing that awareness with God. Ask Him to help you in directing or managing that anger. Or you may find yourself concerned about a particular problem in your life. You might offer the problem up to God, and ask His assistance and guidance. If you find that happy thoughts or feelings fill your present moment, share them with God, adding a brief prayer of thanks. Be sure to time yourself, allowing the full sixty seconds and no more.

This modest exercise, repeated over and over during the day, alters your pattern of busily "doing things." It also is a reminder of the constant closeness and accessibility of God.

Don't read on until you have had a one-minute conversation with God.

Choosing the spiritual exercise right for you at a given time in your day depends on your temperament, your circumstances, and your personal religious background. Whatever exercise you choose to begin with must seem comfortable to you. There is not much point in forcing yourself into a form of devotion absolutely alien to your experience. For example, the Southern Baptist wouldn't feel comfortable spending sixty seconds reciting the Hail Mary, any more than the Catholic would be at ease shouting a hearty "Amen!" during a sermon. Christians are raised with styles of worship that differ from those of other Christians, and it makes sense to respect your own background and taste. If you begin with a one-minute exercise that feels very much "like home," you may find that you can eventually stretch your boundaries to include new and perhaps challenging forms of prayer.

One-Minute Spiritual Exercise 3: Reciting a Familiar Prayer

Begin with a review of the present moment. Then shift to the recitation of a familiar or favorite prayer, perhaps recalled from childhood. There is a comforting quality in the familiar, in the well-known prayer. Allow yourself exactly sixty seconds of that comfort.

Don't read on until you've spent one minute reciting a familiar prayer.

The Psalms are the oldest recorded hymns in the heritage of the church. Written to be sung or read aloud, they have given voice to the fears, hopes, and longings of Jews and Christians alike for many centuries. In many monastic communities the shared singing of psalms is a central act of worship. One of the strongest images many people hold of the religious life is that of monks and nuns singing the Psalms in the ancient plainsong, Gregorian chant.

Traditional and modern hymns continue the heritage of the Psalms. The psalmist pleads with God (Psalms 61:2–3):

> To the rock too high for me,
> > lead me!
> For you are my refuge,
> > a strong tower against the enemy.

The familiar hymn by Martin Luther reflects the same concern:

> Rock of Ages, cleft for me,
> Let me hide myself in thee.

One-Minute Spiritual Exercise 4: Saying Psalms, Singing Hymns

This one-minute exercise not only centers you in the presence of God, but also ties you in with the historical worshiping body of the church. It involves, as before, a brief review of the present moment, followed by one minute of reading from the Psalms or singing a hymn. In the psalm or hymn you share the prayer of many generations of Christians who have preceded you on this path.

Review your present moment. What are you aware of thinking, feeling, or doing? Now let the psalmist help you give voice to your love of God, your trust in Him, by reading aloud the following selection from the Sixty-third Psalm. There is a special value in the *sound* of poetic prayer, and reading aloud permits the poetry to act on your senses as well as on your mind. (When you do this exercise on your own, as part of your personal rule, you may choose any passage from the Psalms, or you may decide to sing a favorite hymn out loud. The psalm offered here is presented as a first experience in one-minute poetic prayer.)

God, you are my God, I am seeking you,
my soul is thirsting for you,
my flesh is longing for you,
a land parched, weary and waterless;
I long to gaze on you in the Sanctuary,
and to see your power and glory.

Your love is better than life itself,
my lips will recite your praise;
all my life I will bless you,
in your name lift up my hands;
my soul will feast most richly,
on my lips a song of joy and, in my mouth, praise.

On my bed I think of you,
I meditate on you all night long,
for you have always helped me.
I sing for joy in the shadow of your wings;
my soul clings close to you,
your right hand supports me.

Psalms 63:1–7

Don't read on until you have said a psalm aloud.

The first Christian monks were the desert fathers, who sought silence and solitude in the deserts of Egypt, Syria, and Palestine in the third through the sixth centuries. They practiced a particularly simple inward discipline. Called Hesychasm, it involved an inner quiet (we'll have more to say about that in chapter 7), and a constant focusing of the mind on God. The monks would inwardly recite short prayers, often as short as the name "Jesus," or "Help me, Lord," over and over with each waking breath, during very long periods of prayer. More recently, Chris-

33

tians in the West have been introduced to the ancient practice of Eastern Orthodoxy—the tradition of the "Jesus Prayer," the constant repetition of "Lord Jesus Christ, Son of the Living God, have mercy on me, a Sinner."

Both of these traditions call for unceasing repetition of the chosen phrase or short prayer. This device can be modified to fit the isolated minutes made free for prayer by your personal rule. Choose a short phrase that carries a special meaning for you. It may be one of those mentioned above, or any other phrase drawn from Scripture, such as the declaration of faith made by Thomas upon seeing the risen Christ: "My Lord and my God" (John 20:28).

One-Minute Spiritual Exercise 5: Repeating a Brief Devotional Phrase or Prayer

Choose a prayer or phrase from the examples given above, or select any other prayer or phrase whose meaning is special to you. We suggest a shorter modification of the Jesus Prayer: A word or a phrase chosen from Scripture, such as Jesus, Abba, Yahweh, Come Lord Jesus, or Father. Check your watch or clock, then relax, breathing slowly and comfortably. Begin with a brief review of your present moment. Then, as you continue to breathe slowly, repeat your word or phrase with each exhalation. Continue for one minute.

Don't read on until you have spent one minute repeating a brief phrase or prayer.

Once you have chosen an exercise that suits you, begin to fit it into your daily living according to your personal rule of life. None of these prayers will change your life in one minute. They are not magic words, Christian abracadabras, bearing the promise of instant fulfillment of whatever wish you may have in mind. But each of them serves to push aside the stream of busy, ordinary, crisis-management thinking, and makes an opening in your mind for God's entry. Once you have let Him into your life, His work through you can begin in earnest. There is no more for the Christian to ask.

5 · The One-Minute Scripture Meditation

It may often seem that God is silent; that His presence in your life is difficult to discern.

The written Word provides a point of certain contact with God. God is always available through Scripture, which Isaiah describes as rain that falls upon the earth, bringing forth new growth and sustaining life. In order to grow in the Spirit, this rainfall must come into the deserts of human life.

> Yes, as the rain and the snow come down from the heavens and do not return without watering the earth, making it yield and giving growth to provide seed for the sower and bread for the eating, so the word that goes from my mouth does not return to me empty, without carrying out my will and succeeding in what it was sent to do. (Isaiah 55:10–11)

Most of us actually read very little Scripture, because the Bible can be a difficult book. We read most books by starting on the first page and taking the pages in order until we've finished the book. Unfortunately, failure is almost assured in reading the Bible that way. Most people who set out to read it from cover to cover make it through the desert with Moses and his little band, only to become lost somewhere in the rules about preparation of sacrificial animals and the number of poles in the canopy of a sanctuary tent. It can be hard for the twentieth-century Christian to see what these ancient laws have to do with present reality. So the bookmark ends up somewhere in Leviticus, or Numbers, and the Bible ends up back on the shelf.

There is just too much of the Bible. The merest glance will tell you that it is a long book; and it's not just long; it is also richly complex. Each of its many sections can be understood on at least three levels. At the surface is the history of a group of scattered nomadic families that became a powerful nation, with particular emphasis on the story of a teacher who grew up in that nation during a period of foreign domination. The Bible can be read as history, and seen as no more than a loosely related group of tales about the Jews in the ancient Middle East.

At the second level lies the meaning that the people of those distant times saw in the events of their lives. The Israelites viewed their history as the unfolding of the Covenant, their special relationship with God. Later, in the New Testament, the men and women around Jesus watched him destroy and then rebuild their system of thinking about how to live with their fellow man, and with God. In many ways we model our ideas about God on the conceptions of those people of long ago.

At the third level we find the special meaning that those biblical events have for us in our own time. Paul wrote to the struggling Christian communities of Corinth and Rome, yet his words also speak to the struggling Christian communities of Duluth, Moscow, Sydney, and Hong Kong. The Scriptures say things to us that they could not possibly have said to the people of other times.

This situation is not unique in our generation of Christians—it's been true of all readers of the Bible since the stories were first passed down. Each of us draws special meanings from the individual words, phrases, and stories of the Scriptures. The context of our own day-to-day experience inevitably influences what the Bible means to

37

us. The person who lives and works on a farm will find it relatively easy to relate directly to Christ's parables about sheep and vineyards. Those who have been involved in long-term construction projects (such as a church building program) can appreciate how hard it must have been for the people of Jerusalem to believe Jesus when he said that he would destroy the temple and rebuild it in three days.

Before the present generation, the Bible was never read by people for whom the possibility of nuclear war was a daily reality. Jesus' words about being prepared for the return of the Master in the middle of the night have a new meaning now that any sunset might be the last for all mankind. We are different from the Jews of Isaiah's time, different from the reformers of Luther's day. The Scriptures speak to us within the framework of *our* lives. It can be no other way.

No one can hope to absorb all of the Bible in one sitting or in one week or in one year. It is not just a book to be read or a task to be completed. Perhaps it is better to approach your reading of the Bible as a lifelong conversation with God. You would not sit down with a good friend for one long discussion and imagine that once it stopped, you would never have anything else to say to each other. Instead, you talk with your friend again and again, each time bringing new experiences to the conversation and drawing new learning from the exchange. To use Isaiah's analogy of the rain, it does not make sense to expect that one long downpour could provide all the water that would ever be needed. Scripture is certainly like rainfall in this regard; when there is too much of it, it just runs off. What is needed is the right amount of rain, at the right time and in the right places. The one-minute Scripture meditation is designed to assure a steady exposure to the word of God, at a rate that will allow it to soak in.

The goal is to read and absorb a small amount of the Bible each day. You can easily read a little of the Bible at a time, and in this way read a great deal of it over a period of weeks and months. Matthew has twenty-eight chapters, each of which contains two or three different episodes or short sections. Reading a single episode each day means taking about three months to move through this Gospel. Following this pattern, all four Gospels can be read and digested in a single year.

A fast reader could easily read the entire New Testament in one weekend—but probably by the next weekend, it would be mostly forgotten. Slow but steady reading of Scripture allows the reader to think about each episode, letting the events and their meanings soak in. When you read a novel, the major interest is the direction of the story: Where is it going? How will it end? You already know that the path of Jesus leads to Jerusalem, and you know how his earthly journey ends. The important issues in this story are often found in the twists and turns along the road.

You will need a plan to guide your reading of the Bible. Some people sit down, let the Bible fall open, and then begin reading whatever they find. This is like taking all the pills in your house—the vitamins, the medicines, the dog's worm tablets—and pouring them into a big paper sack. Then, when for some reason or another you felt the need of a pill, you would reach into the sack and take whatever you pulled out, hoping it would somehow make you feel better.

At the end of a long, trying day you might be lucky enough to open your Bible to Second Corinthians 12:9–10 and find the following:

"My Grace is enough for you: my power is at its best in weakness. So I shall be very happy to make my weaknesses my special boast so that the power of Christ may stay over me, and that is why I am quite content with my weaknesses, and with insults, hardships, persecutions, and the agonies I go through for Christ's sake. For it is when I am weak that I am strong."

If you were not so fortunate, at the end of the same difficult day you might let your Bible fall open and find yourself reading the following passage from Joshua 17:1–4:

> A portion was awarded by lot to Manasseh, because he was Joseph's first-born son. To Machir, Manasseh's eldest son and father of Gilead, there fell, as was right for a fighting man, the country of Gilead and Bashan. And portions were also given to Manasseh's other sons, according to their clans: to the sons of Abiezer, the sons of Helek, the sons of Asriel, the sons of Shechem, the sons of Hepher, the sons of Shemida: these were the clans of the male children of Manasseh son of Joseph. Zelophehad son of Hepher, son of Gilead, son of Machir, son of Manasseh, had no sons, only daughters, whose names are these: Mahlah, Noah, Hoglah, Milcah and Tirzah. (Joshua 17:1–4)

Both of these readings are from Scripture. Both contain elements of the story of the Jewish people and the Christian understanding of salvation through grace. But one provides considerable comfort and direction, and the other very little.

Random selection is a poor way to choose Scripture passages. If you are looking for a reading to meet a special need, you are likely to be disappointed with the results. Random selection will take you willy-nilly to the Gospel of John one day, to one of the lamenting psalms on the next, and to the story of Moses on the third day, with no connection or pattern. Such jumping around provides no opportunity to develop any sense of the continuity within the Scriptures. Each event in the Old Testament is an element of an evolving history. Unless you can follow the development of at least a given segment of that history, you are likely to be confused rather than edified. Christ's actions build on one another, and what he does in Jerusalem will be easier to understand in light of his earlier ministry in Galilee.

A number of ready-made resources for choosing readings can provide pattern and continuity for your readings, while exposing you to the wide variety of the Scriptures. Any religious bookstore will have a number of books offering a selected daily Scripture reading, usually accompanied by a brief commentary. There are many excellent Bible study guides that explore one book of the Bible at a time, providing both selected readings and additional information about each reading and its meaning.

If you belong to a Christian tradition that celebrates daily Eucharist, you are likely to have available a book that gives the daily readings to be used at the Communion service. In the Episcopal Church this is *The Book of Common Prayer*; in the Roman Catholic church the readings are found in the *Daily Missal* or in an *Ordo* (a liturgical resource usually printed by each diocese); in the Lutheran church the readings for the day can be found by consulting The Lutheran Book of Worship.

If none of these ready-made resources seems appealing, you may decide to select one book of the Bible at a time and work your way through it by reading a small section each day.

If you are in a congregation, don't neglect your pastor: He is likely to be very eager to help you find a fruitful direction for your reading. Many clergy report that they end up doing a great deal of marriage counselling and social work, but wish they were called upon more often for spiritual guidance. That is, after all, their basic line of work.

A special augmentation of your personal rule of life is necessary for the one-minute Scripture meditation. It takes most of us at least five minutes to read and absorb even a short section of Scripture, so you need to find a special time for reading the Bible—a single daily period of five undistracted minutes.

Choosing a time rather early in the morning might make it possible for you to meditate on your Scripture reading several times as the day wears on. The reading might come before your first cup of coffee or before breakfast. People who live in large families or in close quarters may find it necessary to get up before the rest of the household in order to be able to give the Bible full attention for five minutes. If you travel to work on a train or bus, you could carry along a pocket Bible and read the Scriptures for five minutes in transit before starting on the usual morning newspaper or work-related reading. A mother who sends her children off to school might find five minutes available right after the children have gone, before she starts her morning tasks.

Remember, the key is to insert your five minutes with the Bible *before* performing your usual *automatic behavior*.

There are four steps to be carried out during the five-minute reading.

1. Read the Bible selection carefully, letting the words settle in. This is not a time for speed reading.

2. Go over the passage in your mind, without looking at it. What did Jesus say? What did the psalmist proclaim about God? What was Paul telling the people of Rome?

3. Read through the selection again, making sure you understood it. It's all too easy to extract from the text what we *want* to have read, rather than what was actually on the page.

In one memorable story (Luke 5:17–26), a crippled man is carried through the crowds by his friends, who hope that Jesus can help him. Unable to get through the press of people around the door, they cut a hole in the roof and lower the paralytic into the room where Jesus is. Jesus first forgives his sins, then cures his crippled body. For years a man well-versed in the Bible carried a clear memory of the cripple being raised *up* through the roof to where Jesus was talking to his disciples and the gathered crowd. Somehow he had acquired the story that way during his childhood, and the memory had stayed with him, completely backward, for thirty years or more. Memory can play tricks, so make a strong effort to store the events correctly.

4. Select a central idea or phrase to help you recall the Scripture passage during the day. Sometimes even a single word jotted down will help you remember the reading.

Scripture Exercise 1: The First Reading of a Passage

Begin by reading through the following passage from the Gospel of Luke, in which John the Baptist preaches to the crowds.

> He said, therefore, to the crowds who came to be baptised by him, "Brood of vipers, who warned you to fly from the retribution that is coming? But if you are repentant, produce the appropriate fruits, and do not think of telling yourselves, 'We have Abraham for our father' because, I tell you, God can raise children for Abraham from these stones. Yes, even now the axe is laid to the roots of the trees, so that any tree which fails to produce good fruit will be cut down and thrown on the fire."
>
> When all the people asked him, "What must we do, then?" He answered, "If anyone has two tunics he must share with the man who has none, and the one with something to eat must do the same." There were tax collectors too who came for baptism, and these said to him, "Master, what must we do?" He said to them, "Exact no more than your rate." Some soldiers asked him in their turn, "What about us? What must we do?" He said to them, "No intimidation. No extortion. Be content with your pay."
>
> Luke 3:7–14

Don't proceed until you have carefully read the passage, letting the words settle in as you read them.

Now that you have completed the first step by carefully reading the selection from Luke's Gospel, go through each of the following steps.

Review the passage mentally, without looking back at the page. Who was speaking, and what did he have to say? How did the listeners respond?

Now, go back and check the passage. Did you get the story right? Be sure to correct any details that might have gotten confused.

Finally, select a central idea or even a single word that will help you remember the passage. Perhaps "brood of vipers" would serve as your reminder, or "John speaks to the crowds." For this exercise, write down the idea or word to help you remember the passage later. Put the piece of paper someplace where you can find it—you'll be making use of it later.

Scripture Exercise 2: Rereading a Favorite Passage

For this exercise you will need a Bible. Turn to a favorite passage. If you are not particularly familiar with the Bible, it may be difficult to find a favorite passage; indeed, you may have to hunt around to find one that sounds familiar. If this is the situation, you will want to make the one-minute Scripture meditation a regular part of your personal rule of life. Having made an argument against random selection of Scripture passages, we won't now suggest that you simply open your Bible and "select" whatever stares up at you. Instead, look into the front of your copy of the Bible, where some editions offer selections for certain situations in life. See whether there's a listing that sounds as if it makes sense for this moment in your spiritual journey.

If your edition does not have such listings, here are a number of selections familiar to almost anyone who has ever attended church.

- The twenty-third Psalm is an Old Testament reading familiar to almost everyone. You might read the entire Psalm in this exercise—it's quite short.
- Ecclesiastes speaks of time and human life in the third chapter of the book that has been given his name. The first eleven verses make a good, brief reading.
- In the New Testament, the first chapter of John's Gospel contains a clear statement of the role of Christ. You might read the first fourteen verses.
- The story of the Prodigal Son is told in Luke 15:11–32.
- Paul's first letter to the Corinthians clearly states the Christian understanding of the place of death in human life. You might want to read the fifteenth chapter of One Corinthians, verses fifty-four through fifty-eight.

Whatever reading you select, either one of your own favorites or one of those suggested above, take the next five minutes and let the word of God, as expressed in the Scripture, soak into your mind. Repeat each of the four steps (discussed earlier in detail):

- First, read through the selection carefully, letting the words settle in as you read them.
- Go over the passage in your mind, without looking at it.
- Read through the selection again to make sure that you remembered it correctly.
- Select a central idea or phrase to help you recall the passage during the day. Write down a single word or more to help you remember the reading.

Don't proceed until you have completed this careful reading and consideration of the Scripture passage you selected.

Reflecting on a Scripture reading as you sit with Bible in hand is easier than trying to remember at the end of a busy day what it was you read that morning. But a word or phrase you've written down will trigger memory in most situations. And in the process you'll be teaching yourself how to read more carefully and retentively.

Scripture Exercise 3: The One-Minute Scripture Meditation

All this preparation has been leading up to one exercise, the one-minute Scripture meditation. If you accept Isaiah's analogy of Scripture and rain, then you know that it is important to bring God's word into contact with your daily life. Like water, the word of God encourages growth.

The one-minute Scripture meditation is designed to be done several times each day. As with the exercises outlined in the previous chapter, you need to identify one or more automatic behaviors and insert this exercise into your day by doing it *before* the automatic behaviors.

Begin the exercise by checking your watch or clock; remind yourself to stick to the sixty-second period. Start with a review of your present situation. Where are you, right here, right now? What are you doing? What are you aware of in your surroundings? What thoughts or feelings come to mind?

After you have reviewed your present moment, look at the word you wrote down to remind yourself of the second reading, *the reading you chose for yourself.* Quickly review the passage in your mind. You do not need to recite it from memory—just go over what it was about. After all, you are trying to accomplish this in one minute!

Before your minute is up, try to find a connection between the reading and your present situation. How does the reading you chose relate to this moment in your spiritual journey? What does God have to say to you right here, right now?

Don't read on until you have completed the one-minute Scripture meditation.

Sometimes the connection between the Bible reading and your immediate experience will be obvious. If you're at a party and the day's reading was the story of the wedding at Cana, it will not be hard to see how the Gospel relates to the present moment. If you are experiencing a time of personal weakness and the reading was the story of the woman in the crowd who was healed by touching Jesus as he passed, the comforting message of the Scripture will touch you. At other times the connection will be hard to find, or will not be there at all. God does not grant us revelations every day, although there are certainly revelations available for each of us to experience. If the connection is not clear, nothing is lost: The important act is *seeking* the connection, looking for a relationship between present experience and the word of God. In this way Scripture ceases to be a collection of stories in a book, and begins to become a conversation with God.

Some passages will clearly call for action in the present situation. Perhaps you will find a call to make an act of witness, or to comfort another. In many situations no action may be clearly called forth. Even then, your experience of the present moment will be changed: For one minute you have focused on the word of God. We are meant to lead our lives differently because of our faith in Christ, who is shown to us in Scripture.

Scripture Exercise 4: Your Second One-Minute Scripture Meditation

It may seem that a lot has gone on since you read the first Scripture exercise passage, from the Gospel of Luke; you've been distracted from the ideas you considered in that reading. Find the piece of paper with the corresponding word or phrase jotted on it—we told you that we'd ask you to retrieve it.

Now, use that key word or key phrase to unlock your memory of the reading from Luke, and carry out the one-minute Scripture meditation, minding your watch or clock as you go through the steps. Inventory your present moment, call the Scripture reading to mind, and then look for a connection between the reading and your present experience. Remember, this is to be done in about sixty seconds.

Don't read on until you have completed this exercise.

When the one-minute Scripture meditation is carried out several times each day, as designed, each repetition brings the same Scripture into different parts of your day. Returning to Isaiah's theme, we may reflect that rain does no good unless it falls where it's needed. The one-minute Scripture meditation brings the rain of Scripture into the places in our lives where we need it.

As long as the Bible is but a big book on a shelf, it's not of much use. Once it becomes a part of your life, you can begin to experience the Bible as a meaningful part of your experience of the presence of God. The prophet said that the word does not return empty, but accomplishes the purposes of the Father. The goal of the one-minute Scripture meditation is to bring the word into our lives, so that God's purposes can be accomplished in us and through us.

6 · Sharing Prayer: Brief Exercises within Community Worship

Going to church is important. Individual prayer opens lives to God; shared worship draws our separate lives together into a new being, the worshiping body of the church. Praying in common, we are a palpable reminder, to ourselves and others, of Christ's continuing presence in the world.

Tennis players like to get together to talk tennis, and wine lovers go to meetings to discuss the virtues of their favorite vintages. Committed Christians need to go to church, and there share their faith.

In a society that so highly values the practical utility of things, it's easy to underestimate the value of Sunday worship. New Christians, especially those who come into the church as adults, are delightedly (and delightfully) aware of the spiritual power and beauty of shared worship.

However, for some Christians, churchgoing has become a matter of routine—familiar, predictable, and even boring. Attendance can become a habit, or even worse, an empty ritual performed out of a sense of obligation; the would-be worshiper develops a "time clock" mentality, and unconsciously punches in at the beginning of the service, punches out at the end. And this in spite of one's best intentions.

Community Worship Exercise 1: Personal Reasons for Going to Church

There are many reasons for going to church. Take a piece of paper and a pencil, and write down all of the reasons you went to church *whenever you last attended*. List both the noble and the not-so-noble reasons. If you went out of habit, say so. If you went to pray about a specific issue, list that as well.

Now, make a complete and honest list of the reasons you skipped services *the last Sunday that you did not attend*.

Write your list of reasons before you read on.

Social forces that once sent people into the churches on Sunday are rapidly eroding. Once upon a time, someone who stayed home on Sunday morning was considered suspect—not the sort of person one would want to hire or to have as a son-in-law. People attend church for a variety of reasons, some more elevated than others, but there is no longer much social pressure favoring churchgoing. The direction of the pressures may even have reversed: In certain circles, religious people are considered a bit behind the times, less sophisticated than those who have replaced Sunday services with brunch and a game of tennis.

Eventually many people who have attended mainly out of habit or fear become fed up with the entire performance, and stop going altogether. Not uncommonly, people say, "I still believe in God, but I just don't go to church." Although, sadly, the feeling is understandable, that's much like saying, "I believe in medicine, I just don't go to doctors." There are many good reasons to go to church. But to fully appreciate the richness of shared worship, one must remove the blinders of familiarity and take another look at community worship.

Going to church in our times can be a highly significant

act. Many Christians who go to church today are there thanks to their faith that something very important happens during the service. Their vital, committed presence says that they belong to the church, that they have chosen to be members of the worshiping body of Christians.

Community Worship Exercise 2: Remembering Special Moments in Worship

Some Sundays are special: The service, the sermon, and the surroundings all come together in a beautiful way. On those days our experience of the church is very strong. Close your eyes and recall a time when worship was special. Perhaps it was last week, or it may have been thirty years ago. Now spend one minute remembering the experience.

Spend a minute recalling a special time of worship before you read on.

Shared public worship provides the enduring structure, the backbone of Christian spirituality. The weekly service is the major religious experience in the lives of most Christians. It is a public drama, a recital of "the mighty acts of God." In words largely unchanged since the days of the apostles, we retell the story of God's entry into our world and into our lives. We speak of our faith that Christ has made us different people and that our lives are better because of those changes. We pray, and praying together demonstrates the faith that our prayers are heard.

The ancient words and rituals speak of our ties to the Christian people who came before us; of our hopes for those Christians who will continue to repeat the services long after we are gone. Coming together for worship, we join with our brothers and sisters in the many churches and denominations throughout the world. Our prayers and

51

our concerns are mingled with those of Christians worshiping in African huts and in European cathedrals, in the presence of queens and presidents and in secret, hidden places. We are joined in prayer with the wealthy and the starving, with those in quiet suburban neighborhoods and those in the rubble of bombed-out villages.

Our common faith, expressed in our worship, makes us all one.

The independent development of liturgy in various cultures and settings led to many different styles of Christian community worship. This diversity has both good and bad aspects. It has allowed the development of varying patterns of worship that are comfortable and meaningful for many varying groups of people. However, we tend to perceive people who do things differently as doing them incorrectly. Differences in style have become sources of deep division.

Nevertheless, in our century there is a powerful movement bringing the denominations together, blurring the artificial lines between us. Sunday worship services in most churches have come to resemble one another far more than the average churchgoer realizes. In the United States there are striking similarities in worship among the Catholic, Episcopal, Protestant, and Evangelical communities.

Even more impressive is the remarkable convergence in basic doctrine, worship, and spirituality now taking place within the worldwide Christian community. The many churches are rediscovering that they are the Church. Old wounds are healing, painful divisions are ending— and nowhere is the healing more evident than in public worship, the Sunday service. This is not to say that there are no longer differences: The order of the service followed by an Eastern Orthodox congregation does not superficially resemble that familiar to Missouri Synod Lutherans. The diversity of expression continues, but with a renewed appreciation for commonality.

Shared worship is more formal and structured than individual prayer. Instead of praying about whatever comes

52

to mind, one joins in a service that is dictated by custom and is largely under the direction of someone else. During such formal prayer it is easy to drift off into thoughts about a sixteen-year-old daughter's driving, a son's Little League team, the problems in one's marriage, or perhaps the chances of one's getting a promotion.

There is no way for anyone to pay absolute attention to every moment in an entire worship service. However, there are ways to become a more active participant, to enter more deeply into the service and draw more out of it. There is a difference between just going to church and truly *being* there.

The goal of the following exercises is to enrich the experience of shared worship. By taking a new look at the service, you can draw back the curtains of familiarity that sometimes make it hard to see the spiritual riches inherent in community worship. Each of the exercises can be used in a variety of worship settings. They were designed so that differences in the style of community worship will not render the exercises useful in the services of only one denomination or another. They are to be done in church, during services.

A number of the exercises begin with an inventory of the present moment. In shared worship, the present moment consists of your own experience *and* whatever is happening in the worship service. The liturgy goes ahead at its own pace, without waiting for the individual to keep up. To be in tune with the service, you must be aware of the action of the church right now, at this point of worship.

Community Worship Exercise 3: Inventorying the Present Moment in Shared Prayer

This exercise does not take more than a few seconds, but it can have a surprising impact on how you look at things during worship. Do it whenever you feel a need to increase your involvement in the service. In such a moment, take a deep breath, close your eyes, and ask yourself the following questions:

- What am I doing, *right now?*
- What are we doing together in the service, *right now?*

The answer to the first question obviously depends upon what you were just doing. You may have been reading the bulletin, looking for the date of the potluck supper. Perhaps your attention had drifted to the inscriptions on the stained glass windows, or the lovely new jacket on the lady in the front pew.

On the other hand, you may be thinking about something the preacher had to say during her message that morning. If you are involved in the service at the time of the inventory, that will be very clear. (And you'll have acquired more evidence that it's possible for your mind to do at least two things at once.)

If you were thinking about something outside your spiritual life, become aware of the fact—but don't scold yourself for a wandering mind. First, it's natural. Second, awareness causes change. Noticing absentmindedness often brings increased attention.

Answering the second question requires not only observation, but an understanding of the nature of the service as well. Each moment in a service has its own purpose, its own drama, its own contribution to the act of worship. The opening prayers set a tone or a theme, which is often carried through the entire service. In prayers of confession, the worshipers make a public acknowledgment of their own sinfulness and the insufficiency of their efforts, followed by a reassurance of acceptance by a loving God. There are prayers in which the gathered community asks for specific benefits or blessings. These are the prayers of all the people, and of each of the people.

In the Scripture readings, Christians recount their history, their common calling to be people of God, and the shared hope of the Kingdom. Sermons are formal teachings of the church by those chosen as leaders. Psalms and hymns are shared prayer in poetry and music. In the offertory, we symbolically place our lives in God's hands to be transformed and renewed. When the Eucharist is celebrated, the congregation joins in a profound affirmation that Jesus is the Resurrection and the Life, that with him everything is more than what appears to human eyes. In the final blessing, we recall our commission to go into the world, carrying the Good News.

Nothing is surprising in this list of the major actions in worship. It is all familiar, all the stuff of childhood Sunday school or catechism lessons. When things are so familiar, we tend to lose sight of their profundity. The point of this exercise is to recognize the nature and purpose of an action of the church as it unfolds in the present moment of worship. That recognition is a key to fuller participation. We have said the words so many times that we can forget the precious essence of their message. Become conscious. Hear yourself as an individual and the congregation as a body. Notice what you are doing.

Community Worship Exercise 4: Changing the Subject

This exercise—which consists of intentional daydreaming, letting the mind wander on purpose—can be done at any point, whenever attention begins to drift. During any sustained mental activity, you'll experience movement into and then back out of concentration. Sometimes it helps to exaggerate this movement, to pull as far away from the service as possible, then to swing back, coming deeper into the center of the act of worship.

When you become distracted during the service, close your eyes and take a deep breath. Begin this exercise the same way as the first, reviewing the present moment through answering the following questions:

- What am I doing, *right now?*
- What are we doing together in the service, *right now?*

Then, let your mind wander. Daydream, have a fantasy about being someplace else, doing something else. Take thirty seconds or so to let the daydream develop. Try to enter the fantasy fully, developing sensory images of vision, sound, touch, or even scent. Notice what is happening in the daydream. After about thirty seconds, try to identify the most important thing going on in the fantasy—the central event or feeling of it. Then return to the service.

The daydream is likely to provide a reminder of something that needs attention in prayer.

Perhaps the most important thing in the daydream is something going on at work. There may be problems on the job; they can be brought into the worship as concerns to set before God. Or you may have questions about the direction of a career for which you need guidance. On the other hand, there may be special graces in your work for which thanks should be offered.

The central image in the daydream might have been another person. Try to become aware of your feelings about that person within the daydream. Those feelings may indicate concerns you have about the other person; or they may be your response to certain qualities in the person that you especially appreciate. Bring along those thoughts when reentering the worship service. Perhaps there are some special prayers needed for the other person or for the relationship you share.

After you turn your attention back to the service, the thoughts begun during the daydream will continue, altering your experience of worship. We often drift away from the service when it seems that what is going on is not related to "real life." The daydream reflects the concerns that shape your day-to-day life. When those concerns are made a part of the act of worship, either through prayer or through simple reflection, Sunday and the rest of the week are brought face to face. Any artificial lines you've drawn between what you may have felt to be separate parts of life begin to fade and blur.

Community Worship Exercise 5: Stepping into Participation

This is another exercise for times when the mind wanders. Look around the room. Notice the faces, the gestures, the visible actions of both the congregation and the clergy. Then review the present moment by asking the same two questions:

- What am I doing *right now?*
- What are we doing together in the service, *right now?*

After the review of the present moment, make a conscious effort to join in the work of prayer. The task here is simple. Identify what the congregation is doing, and then do it along with them. If the congregation is giving thanks, give thanks yourself. Go through your list of blessings and express your gratitude to God. If the congregation is confessing sinfulness, take that moment to focus on a specific personal sin, one that continues to be a problem. Recognize the distance that your negative thoughts and actions create between you and God. As the assurance of forgiveness is pronounced, commit yourself to reduce the divisions in your life by changing the behaviors that create them.

Enter into the action of the congregation. Become active rather than merely present.

Community Worship Exercise 6: Writing Your own Sermon

The sermon is an important part of most services, and the center of many services in which the Eucharist is not

57

celebrated. Some sermons are captivating, making concentration simple. It's easy to be involved because the
speaker carries the congregation along.

Even the best preachers have off days, of course, and
others seem to make a habit of being terribly dull. In such
a situation, being involved with the sermon takes work.

If the sermon leaves you cold, write a better one. Instead
of writing your grocery list, quickly review the readings
for the day, or the text chosen for the sermon. Then
mentally outline what you would say if given the podium.
How would you approach the theme of the gospel reading?
What message stands out in the epistle? Which examples
would make the sermon more personal and lively?

Writing an alternative to the sermon being given will
help you think about the readings and the theme of the
day's service. Some of what the preacher has to say could
turn out to make sense after all, and in any case the
exercise brings a new appreciation of the difficulty of pre-
paring clear and meaningful sermons. This exercise will
also assure that some part of the message sinks in.

Community Worship Exercise 7: Really Singing the Hymns

Saint Augustine said that a person who sings hymns prays
twice, once with the words and once with the music.
Music involves the senses and the emotions in the act of
prayer. You can employ a number of devices to increase
your involvement in the singing of hymns. Each focuses
on a different aspect of the complex experience of singing
hymns. These exercises are different from the preceding
ones in that they do not begin with a review of the present
moment. They are meant to be done as you sing along,
enhancing your participation in the hymn without first
interrupting it.

Upon recognizing the first few chords of a familiar an-
them, the listener is already involved in the prayer of the
hymn. Even before the words begin, the music calls forth

memories. In its own wordless way, the melody brings up long-forgotten times, people, and places. Singing your mother's favorite hymn inevitably brings back feelings from childhood. Perhaps the hymns you sang at 4-H or church camp are reminders of the emotions and thoughts that accompanied those early adventures in independence. Hymns sung in college may be bound up with memories of love's first heady days. Sometimes hymns bring up sad memories as well, such as the feelings that come with a hymn strongly tied to a memory of a lost loved one. One of the authors still feels waves of grief whenever he hears a certain song that was sung at the wedding of a brother later killed in an automobile accident.

While singing a familiar hymn, focus awareness on the feelings elicited by the melody. Let the memories flow into your consciousness as you sing. Sometimes one cannot even recall what specific earlier event ties the music you're hearing with the emotion you suddenly feel again in the present: Music bypasses thought in its direct ties to emotion.

As you sing a familiar hymn, your personal history becomes a part of the poetry, blended into the prayer. Recognize and honor your emotions—they are an important part of spiritual life. Offer them to God, along with the words of the hymn.

Not all hymns are familiar, but all are poetic prayer. Sometimes the poetry can be very moving, clearly expressing our hopes and fears. At other times the imagery expresses a concept about God more clearly than a twenty-page theological treatise ever could. For example, consider the following single lines from familiar hymns:

'tis only the splendor of light hideth Thee.

or this line from an old standard:

Early in the morning, our song shall rise to Thee.

59

or this stanza from a children's hymn:

All things bright and beautiful,
All creatures great and small,
All things wise and wonderful,
The Lord God made them all.

In singing any hymn, attend to what the poet is saying through the lyrics. Perhaps there will be a single line, or a single verse, that's "just right" in its expression of a feeling or an idea. Take that line or verse into your mind, and let it settle there.

Finally, in singing the prayer, all in the congregation are bound together by rhythm and melody. Listen to the sound of the voices singing together. Then let your voice, your prayer, mingle with the voices and the prayers of the people around you. Appreciate the manifest unity that is shared song.

Community Worship Exercise 8: Remembering the Others

In community worship we pray not only with other members of the congregation, but with all Christians. Often the formal prayer of the congregation calls to mind the many members of the church in the world, praying for the special concerns of certain groups. This exercise is designed to help us remember the others.

Begin with a review of the present moment. Then look about and find an empty spot in a nearby pew. In your imagination, put someone in the pew, a friend who is not in church today. Take a moment and pray for this friend, perhaps asking God's help for a specific known problem. Next, bring in someone whom you do not particularly like. Offer for God's attention this person's needs and concerns as well. Now, from your imagination or from today's newspaper, bring in a stranger—perhaps someone in or from another country, an African Christian or a

Christian from Russia. Lift up the concerns of faraway people in your prayers. It is easy to reach into the past, and bring in a remembered loved one, or even further, and carry into your congregation one of the Christians from the Middle Ages, or even one of the disciples. Little by little, fill your church with invisible Christian brothers and sisters. Try to imagine what they would look like, and what it would be like actually to have them present. And remember that their concerns are also your concerns. We are the many members of one body.

Shared worship is a central part of Christian life. It is easy to participate—just go to church. And yet full participation can also be very difficult because the familiarity of the service leads to lost excitement and to complacency. It becomes all too easy to go through the prescribed motions, missing out on the inexhaustible spiritual richness of our traditional services. In community prayer we are challenged to make the old new again. This is the unending challenge of all Christian life.

7 · The Prayer of Silence: Quiet Time Alone in the Presence of God

Silence is rare in our lives. We are accustomed to the sounds of people talking, a radio playing, an automobile driving by. Airplanes fly noisily overhead. Dogs bark and neighbors argue. Busy people are generally surrounded by sound—sound produced by children, other adults, and of course the television set. And then, at the prospect of a moment of peace, the telephone rings.

Countless sources of sound guarantee lives sufficiently filled with noise. But we do not seem content to suffer those alone; it is as though we fear the potential dangers of exposure to silence, and therefore seek to drive the last remnant of quiet from our lives. Every automobile has a radio, and many have cassette players as well. Is our living room complete without a stereo system, a television set, a video tape recorder, and three beeping electronic games? Millions of people cannot fall asleep in a quiet environment, so the bedside table holds a clock radio that turns the music off *after* the listener is safely dreaming. The well-equipped recreational vehicle has a generator on the roof so that the occupants need not miss out on prime-time TV just because they happen to be camping somewhere in the mountains. Finally, the battery-powered tape recorder/player now insures that the top 40 can be heard with astounding clarity even deep in the wilderness. If silence is a demon, it has been successfully exorcised from our lives.

Exercise 1 in Silence: Listening to the Sounds Around You

Many of us are so used to the surrounding noise that we almost don't hear it anymore. Take one minute and listen to your surroundings. Close your eyes and become aware of the sounds that push back the silence.

Don't read on until you have spent one minute listening.

What if silence is a treasure? What if there is something in the silence of the desert that made the Middle East the cradle of Christian spirituality? Perhaps we have lost out on a precious experience by filling every moment with aural distraction. Maybe in silence it is easier to hear the voice of God.

Christianity has a long history of men and women actively seeking silence, a time of quiet in prayer. Our Lord himself often withdrew from the din of his followers. Before launching his ministry in Galilee, he went out into the desert, seeking silence and a confrontation with the power of good and evil. Many times during the period of active teaching, Christ led his disciples away from the crowds for solitude and prayer. Finally, before his arrest and trial in Jerusalem, he retired alone in the silence of Gethsemane, face to face with the Father. Ever since, Christian believers have followed his path into quiet retreat. What is there about silence that has led these people to seek what so many of us seem bent on avoiding?

Exercise 2 in Silence: Remembering a Time of Silence in Your Own Life

Perhaps there have been occasions in your own life when you sought out silence, or when you accidentally found yourself alone in quiet, peaceful surroundings. Spend a minute recalling one of these times of silence. What was silence like for you? Can you imagine being back in that quiet time? Try to remember the situation clearly, visualizing and otherwise sensing as many of its aspects as possible.

Don't read on until you have spent one minute recalling a time of silence in your own life.

You may have been comfortable and happy in silence. On the other hand, it may have made you nervous, anxious to have somebody to talk to or something to do. When silence is a new experience, it can seem odd and foreign, even painful. It takes a while to get used to quiet, but once familiar, it can become addictive; one actively seeks it.

The spiritual value of silence lies in the absence of distractions. God is always present, available to us in each moment. But with so much noise in our lives, we often fail to apprehend His presence. God does not become more present in silence; but in silence we're more likely to notice that He is there.

We've mentioned the first Christian monks, the desert fathers of the fourth and fifth centuries. These men and women (the traditional term includes both sexes) did not just flirt with silence—they made a radical commitment to silence as a way of life. They sought God by living in tiny communities in caves and huts scattered about the deserts of Egypt, Syria, and Palestine. They saw any bodily or social comfort as a barrier deflecting one's attention from its proper focus on God. Silence was among the highest of their values. Again and again, their recorded sayings state that closeness to God is found in the individual's lonely confrontation with silence and solitude. "Flee the world, be silent and pray always." These were the keys to the spirituality of the desert fathers.

The desert fathers have had a profound impact on Christian spiritual life ever since. Their teachings on the need for silence, retreat from the concerns of the everyday world, and meditation on the Scriptures set the pattern for much of traditional Christian spiritual life. The great Western religious communities—such as the Franciscans, Dominicans, and Benedictines—all draw from the ideals advanced by these spiritual pioneers in the desert. The influence of their thinking is very evident in the spiritual character of Eastern Orthodoxy. In addition, much of the Protestant Reformation was directed toward moving this personal spirituality out of the monastic setting and into the lives of ordinary people.

A common aspect of the spiritual life is a search for silence, for an undistracted point of view from which to see God. Prayer that grows directly out of the search for silence is called contemplative prayer. In contemplative prayer the mind becomes silent, quietly focused on the present reality of God. Contemplative prayer is not an act—it is more a state of being. The contemplative is not doing anything special in order to maintain the awareness of God's presence; rather, he or she has stopped doing things that detract from that awareness. When the contemplative achieves true silence, only God remains.

The desert fathers called this true silence hesychia: stillness, quiet, and tranquillity. Hesychia implies four levels of silence.

First is silence of the surroundings. The desert fathers fled to the desert to be away from the distractions and noises of the towns and villages.

Second is silence of the voice. The desert fathers felt that superfluous words were a source of sin. Certainly, it is difficult to listen to anyone—whether to one's neighbor or to God—while one is speaking.

Third is silence of the mind. In order to concentrate one's attention on God, the desert fathers believed it necessary to silence the constant inner chatter of thought. Most of us find it difficult even to imagine how one would stop thinking. It seems as though to be human is to be constantly engaged in mental activity, self-address. But it is possible to learn ways to make the mind be quiet.

Fourth is silence of the will. The desert fathers taught that the only way to become fully attuned to the will of God was to stop wanting things for yourself. To a society in which "looking out for number one" has become an article of secular faith, this aspect of silence is perhaps the most difficult to attain.

The desert fathers set a high standard for silence, one that is perhaps unattainable by the busy twentieth-century Christian. After all, few of us are likely to go into monasteries, and even fewer are likely to seek the solitude of the desert. But our way of life need not cut us off entirely from the spiritual benefits of silence.

The prayer of silence is an exercise based on the teachings of the desert fathers. Its name expresses the goal—a quiet awareness of God's presence. Descriptions of this form of prayer are found in Christian writings from the desert fathers through the ages, to the most contemporary Christian spiritual authors. Similar exercises are found in other religious traditions, and over the last twenty years transcendental meditation, a Hindu form of quiet prayer, has gained much attention and acceptance in the West. Finally, some present-day physicians and psychologists teach mental focusing techniques for stress management, offering exercises stripped of religious or spiritual intent. (The techniques are not necessarily without incidental spiritual effect.)

The prayer of silence has taken many forms. What

follows is a basic outline for the prayer, with a number of possible modifications. Although there can be no cut-and-dried formula for achieving the contemplative state, some guidelines can be given for achieving silence of the surroundings and silence of the voice. Suggestions can also be made on achieving silence of the mind. Silence of the will is God's gift—no instructions will be found here. It can only grow out of the maturity of your own prayer life.

- *Silence of the Surroundings*: Absolute silence is not essential. If it were, there would be no hope of success. What is important is an absence of sounds to which *you* must attend. For example, a solid thump emanating from a room full of children is not unusual, nor need it be particularly distracting, *if* someone else is looking after the children! Similarly, a ringing phone is no problem if someone else is there to answer it. But there must be twenty minutes in which the outside world can be all but forgotten.

  Help is likely to be needed in this effort. Even if they are not enthusiastic, fully supportive, most people will not actively interfere with your efforts, and some may be quite helpful. Your spouse may be willing to answer the phone and watch the children. Perhaps a friend or coworker will help keep the world at bay for twenty minutes while you pray. Even with help, it remains difficult for many of us to find regular periods of silence, but doing so is often possible.

  Busy people tend to have openings in their lives in the early morning, around noon, and late in the evening. Some people can wake up twenty minutes before the other members of the family. Prayer might be possible over the lunch hour. You may be able to go off to the bedroom for prayer while the rest of the family is watching TV in the evening, or after they have gone to bed.
- *Silence of the Voice*: As you begin, sit quietly and let

your body relax. Do not lie down—it's too easy to fall asleep. Many people are more able to concentrate with their eyes closed, although others prefer to keep them open. If you prefer your eyes open, focus them on a single spot and let them relax as you maintain a steady gaze.

Start with a moment of verbal prayer, uttered either aloud or silently. The Lord's Prayer is especially appropriate, although other prayers may be substituted. After the moment of verbal prayer, continue sitting in a quiet and relaxed posture and move on to the next part of the exercise, attempting to silence your mind.

- *Silence of the Mind:* This is the tricky part. Left to its own devices, the mind will fill up all available silence with thoughts and ideas, worries and daydreams. One can be very quiet on the outside and full of all sorts of noise on the inside.

  Any number of mental devices have been designed that can help bring silence to your mind. Most fill the mind with repetition of a single, short expression. Consciousness thus occupied with a "mindless" task, a peaceful quiet may overcome worldly awareness, making contemplation possible. The following mental device, very similar to one in an earlier chapter, is given only as an example. A number of other possibilities will be listed later.

  Pay attention to your breathing, noticing what it feels like as you inhale and exhale. Then, begin to inwardly repeat the following phrase from Psalm 123 with each exhalation:

  "I lift my eyes to you."

Continue this repetition for at least five minutes, allowing the single thought to fill your mind.

Unless one is particularly apt at concentrating, distracting thoughts will soon start to intrude. Don't worry about them, because their presence is inevitable. Try to ease them out of your mind by refocusing on the phrase from Scripture. It is likely that as the distracting thoughts become more insistent, you will stop repeating the phrase without knowing that you have done so. As soon as you become aware of this drifting, begin repeating the phrase again. This act, of itself, will reduce the level of distraction.

If the thoughts persist, it may help to inwardly say *no* to them, thus easing them out of your mind. Some people find it helpful to imagine that they are actually pushing the thoughts away, brushing them out of the mind with a visualized motion of the hand. Or you might say to yourself, "I'll worry about that later. Right now I'm praying." Then return immediately to the "mindless" repetition of the phrase from Scripture.

In the beginning it may be difficult to maintain concentration for even five minutes. However, as you become accustomed to silence, it will be easier to retain your focus over longer periods. Eventually you may find it consistently possible to maintain the focus, with the inevitable brief interruptions, for twenty minutes at a time. The twenty-minute period should be seen as a long-term goal.

To find out how long you have been at prayer, check a watch or clock. If you planned to pray for fifteen minutes and have time left, simply close your eyes again and return to your focus phrase. If the time has passed, finish by again repeating (inwardly or aloud) the short prayer with which you began. Do not be in a hurry to stand up; some people become so relaxed that they need a minute or two to get things moving again. Allow yourself to return gradually to your usual level of activity.

Exercise 3 in Silence: The Prayer of Silence

Take five minutes to experience the prayer of silence as outlined above. Don't worry if it seems that you are not doing all that well. Just continue with an open mind, a curiosity about what will happen.

Don't read on until you have spent five minutes with the prayer of silence.

Often one's first exposure to the prayer of silence is pleasant, but it can seem somehow insignificant. It is likely to have been filled with numerous distractions and mental self-interruptions. Silence is new to most of us, but the prayer of silence will develop greater depth with continued application. Christian seekers have done this prayer for many years without exhausting the potential of the experience. Do not be impatient with God. Our response to silence matures and develops with time.

There is a wide variety of other mental devices for bringing about silence of the mind. Choose one that is comfortable for you and has a Scriptural base; Christian prayer needs Christian content. There are Jewish contemplatives and Sufi contemplatives, as well as Hindu and Zen contemplatives. If you wish to remain clearly in the tradition of Christian spirituality, you will do better taking your phrase for focus from the Bible than from the *Tibetan Book of the Dead.*

The possible alternatives to the phrase already given are countless. Any phrase from Scripture or from Christian spiritual writings is appropriate. It should be fairly short, and should express some element of your relationship with God. Particularly appropriate might be words that our Lord spoke while alone in prayer: "You must worship the Lord your God, and serve Him alone." (Luke 4:8); or, "Let it be as You, not I, would have it." (Matthew 26:39).

70

Some people meditate on a single word, such as the name of Jesus, or the Aramaic word *Abba* (Father). A single word can make an excellent focus for the prayer of silence.

Some people find that they are better able to concentrate on a visualization. They may imagine a candle, a cross, or even the hand or the face of Jesus. One woman has reported success in focusing on a mental image of the word *Jesus* being written over and over on a blackboard. There are no limits, so long as the content is Christian.

In Zen contemplation, the focus is often on concepts that may appear to be nonsensical phrases but that nonetheless indirectly express a mystical understanding of the world. For example, beginning Zen students are traditionally asked to imagine the sound of one hand clapping, or the image of one's own face before one's mother was born. Expressions of such concepts, called "koans," provide a mental focus for inner silence. They also trick the mind into thinking in unaccustomed ways, and that can lead to new understandings of the nature of reality and of God. This is a Christian koan composed by one of the authors:

You am./I are.
We be.
Jesus.

Finally it would not be appropriate to discuss the prayer of silence without reference to the rosary. This particularly Catholic form of prayer is strongly rhythmic and includes repetition of brief, familiar prayers. It is highly effective toward achieving inner silence. For centuries faithful Christians have used the rosary as a focal point for contemplative prayer.

Whatever type of mental focus is chosen, the prayer of silence cannot be carried out in sixty seconds. For this or any of the spiritual exercises presented in the next two chapters, longer blocks of time should be set aside for prayer. These exercises require about twenty minutes and are done once or twice each day. Should you decide to make the prayer of silence part of your daily life, make the following modifications in the format of your personal rule of life (as presented in chapter 3).

First, identify one or two times each day when you can pray for twenty minutes without interruption.

Second, identify one or two automatic behaviors that occur regularly most days at about the time when you want to insert twenty minutes of prayer. You may take a shower or a long walk at almost the same time each morning; you may get a cup of coffee at noon each day; or you may like to watch TV at nine o'clock each night. The rule is based upon a commitment to do the longer exercise *before* the selected automatic behavior.

Exercise 4 in Silence: Thinking about Silence in Your Life

This is not a one-minute exercise—it may take some time to think through the issues. Use paper and pencil in answering each of the following questions:

- Does the prayer of silence appeal to you? Some people are excited by the idea; others are not. If you are not highly interested in this type of prayer idea, it is unlikely that you will devote to it the amount of time required.
- Could you really set aside one or two twenty-minute periods for prayer on *most* days? If the time simply is not available, there is no reason to make yourself feel guilty by trying to do the impossible.
- If you answer yes to *both* of the first two questions, take the time now to think through and write a personal rule to make the prayer of silence a part of your life. If you have time but do not find the prayer of silence particularly exciting, come back to this point

72

after reading chapters 8 and 9; you may want to do another of the twenty-minute exercises instead. If there is no possibility of consistent twenty-minute retreats in your life, still you can do the prayer of silence from time to time even though it is not part of a daily routine.

Don't read on until you have answered the three questions above.

Silence has been driven almost totally from our hectic modern lives. With the loss of silence we may have also lost an opportunity to attend to God. Part of our society's spiritual hunger may be a hunger for silence, for a quiet place to contemplate the reality of God. The prayer of silence makes it possible for us to follow Jesus into the desert, to come face-to-face with the Father.

8 · The Twenty-Minute Scripture Meditation

"What if I had been there?"

Every reader of the Bible asks this question at some point. Who has read about Moses without wondering what it was like on the mountaintop? We have all wished for the chance to look in on the Sermon on the Mount or the Last Supper. Many Christians have wondered how they might have reacted to the fear confronting Peter on that dark night in Jerusalem. Perhaps we all envy Thomas, who, despite his prior doubts, actually saw his risen Lord.

We'd understand the Bible's message so much more clearly it seems, if we could have been there to hear the conversations that were not recorded, to witness the many small but telling acts that made up the context of any larger event. We could have seen the faces, could have heard the voices, could have known what the countryside was like, could have— But we cannot. And in spite of the richness of Scriptures, there are many times when the narrative seems flat, impersonal, and distant. The gestures and emotions that make up so much of human experience are often only hinted at. Unlike the journalists of our own time, the writers of the scriptural accounts left out most of the "human interest material." Perhaps partly because the Scriptures, at the time they were written, had to be made terse for portability, we are not told how the

Canaanite woman looked when Jesus cured her daughter. We can only guess at what Elijah thought about having Elisha follow him through the desert, or what Mary experienced at the Annunciation.

However, we can imagine some of these details.

Exercise 1 in Scripture Meditation: Seeing a Face You Have Never Seen

Imagine the face of Mary, the mother of Jesus. Close your eyes and take as long as necessary to develop a clear impression of her features and her expression. Try to get as strong a visual image as possible.

Imagine the face of Mary now, before you read on.

Christians have demonstrated a persistent desire to color in the outlines of scriptural events. This urge has been manifested in medieval times by church art and in our times by biblical epic films. When the human details are added, it becomes easier to relate to the Bible stories, easier to think about the events as things that might have happened to us or in which we might have participated. The key elements of the stories remain unchanged, whether or not we fill in the particulars altogether accurately. Certainly Mary had a face, and when we think about Mary, each of us gives her a different face. What does it matter if the mental image comes from a painting by Titian, from an actress in a Zeffirelli film, or from one's own imagination? The important thing about Mary was that she accepted God's call, that she did not refuse her part in the great movement that was taking place. This perception does not change whether one imagines her looking Semitic, Oriental, or Nordic.

It is possible for each of us to add details to the Scriptures, and in this way make biblical events part of our personal repertoire of Christian memory. We can do this by applying the creative power of imagination to the narratives in the Bible, adding details, seeking out human feelings, exploring what it would have been like to be "there." Nothing about this idea is new or controversial. As will be shown later, it is based on hundreds of years of conservative Christian tradition.

Imagination is a diminished capacity in many adults. Most children have the capacity to imagine, to think of things that are not real and treat them as if they were. Children can jump into a game of "let's be horses" as easily as they jump into the spray of water sprinklers on a hot summer day. At some point in the process of growing up, though, we decide that pretending is not quite legitimate, and we find more "important" employment for our minds. Most of us retain the ability to enter into imagination when we are led to that colorful realm by somebody else—a good novelist, for example, or a hypnotist—but we hardly ever venture there on our own. Such behavior would seem silly, and maybe even abnormal. After all, if we allow our artists and performers to give free rein to imagination, we also expect them to be a bit crazy. For the rest of us, cleaving to the available data seems safer, and so we are left inhabiting a world of computer printouts and television news. Our favorite forms of entertainment—television and the movies—may have artistic and social value, but too rarely do they challenge the imagination. Everything is presented up front, in living color—plot, scenery, blood, gore, and buttocks. There is no need to imagine anything.

Imagination is creative. When we read a novel, we participate in the creation of the story by visualizing the people, their actions, and their surroundings. We are not passive recipients of the words. We actively transform them into our own conceptions in sight and sound and emotion. Certainly the novelist's skill is the catalyst that makes it possible for us to experience a novel as though it were

76

real life. But the novel is incomplete until it has entered the active imagination of a reader. Each reader re-creates the novel, and each does so differently from every other reader, with the characters given different faces, different voices, different sets of unspoken prejudices.

Exercise 2 in Scripture Meditation: Imagination Before and After

Many of us have had the experience of reading a book and then seeing a movie or TV show based on the book. Millions of readers knew the characters of *The Thorn Birds*, *Gone with the Wind*, or *The Spy Who Came In from the Cold* long before they saw the film versions of those stories. Try to recall a time when this happened to you. What was the book? How did you feel about the images in the movie or TV production? Did they fit the pictures you had developed in your own mind as you read the book?

Compare a movie or TV-show conception to that of your own imagination—now, before you read on.

Television and movies can actually limit one's ability to imagine. For example, each of the millions who read Nikos Kazantzakis's allegorical novel *Zorba the Greek* mentally saw a different Zorba do a different dance. However, the millions more who saw the film based on the novel all saw the same actor do the same dance. For them there was only one Zorba; they did not "create" him as readers of the novel did. Perhaps as you did the above exercise, you recalled a similar personal experience. We are often surprised and disappointed when we find that others do not imagine things the same way we do.

Television and the movies seem to have made us dependent on the imagination of others for our mental images of things. When we stop using our own imagination, it gets rusty. Then, when we come upon a sparse narrative like the Bible accounts, it's hard for us to conjure up the sort of detail that would give the events life.

It is important to be able to use creative imagination in dealing with the Scriptures; to personalize them. God intended for us to have a role in creation, in the actual making of things. In the second creation narrative of Genesis, all of the other living creatures are brought to Adam to be given their names. This naming is not mere labelling. The ancient Hebrews saw that naming conferred identity and was clearly a part of the act of creation, which God had chosen to share with humanity. Each of us can play a creative role in drawing knowledge from Scripture. The idea is not to make up a new Bible; the one we have is sufficient. Rather, one can take a Bible story into imagination, interact with it, and create a new and personal understanding of the written passage and its implications.

The exercise described below is traditionally called meditation. Today people are likely to think of meditation as something like the exercise described in the chapter on the prayer of silence; the popularity of transcendental meditation has helped establish that perception. The particular form of meditation presented here was formulated in the sixteenth century by Saint Ignatius of Loyola, the founder of the Jesuit community, and has been used by Christians ever since. It is a much more active mental process than the internal quiet of contemplative prayer.

The exercise takes some time, usually between fifteen and twenty minutes. Through it, the reader actually becomes a participant in the Bible narrative. The one-minute Scripture meditation begins the work of making the Bible part of one's life; this longer exercise can expand and deepen that experience. It is appropriate to any narrative portion of Scripture—anyplace where there is a story going on—as opposed to one of the letters of Saint Paul or the long discourses of the prophets. Meditation is an excellent way to enter into the Bible. We suggest you choose stories because they are easy to visualize. A few examples from the Old Testament: Abraham willing to sacrifice Isaac (Genesis 22:1–13); Joseph sold into slavery in Egypt and the happy outcome of the story (Genesis 37–50); David and Goliath (I Samuel 17); God appearing to Moses in the burning bush (Exodus 3); and the deliverance of the Hebrew people from Egypt (Exodus 11–14).

Examples from the New Testament: Peter's denial of Jesus (Matthew 26:69–75); the parable of the Prodigal Son (Luke 15:11–32); the parable of the Good Samaritan (Luke 10:25–27); and Jesus' appearances after his resurrection to Mary Magdalene, the eleven disciples, and Thomas (John 20).

Exercise 3 in Scripture Meditation: Mary and Martha

The first step is to read a selected scripture passage— slowly, and preferably aloud. Hearing the words seems to help activate the imagination, even if the voice is your own. Read through an entire incident, rather than just a verse or two. As you read, mentally supply the details of the scene. Decide whether the day was sunny or cloudy, and then visualize it that way. Were spring flowers blooming? What did the people look like? What were they wearing? How did they stand as they spoke? In the story that follows, a meal is described. What was served? What did the utensils look like? Read the following account (Luke 10:38–42), slowly and aloud, mentally filling in the details as you read. Take as much time as you need. It may take only fifteen seconds to read this single paragraph— or it may take five minutes.

In the course of their journey he came to a village, and a woman named Martha welcomed him into her house. She had a sister called Mary, who sat down at the Lord's feet and listened to him speaking. Now Martha who was distracted with all the serving said, "Lord, do you not care

79

that my sister is leaving me to do the serving all by myself? Please tell her to help me." But the Lord answered: "Martha, Martha," he said, "you worry and fret about so many things and yet so few are needed, indeed only one. It is Mary who has chosen the better part; it is not to be taken from her."

Step One: Mentally enter the life of one of the characters in the story.

Having read the passage, you will be role-playing the events in your mind. First be Martha, in the same way as in a child's game of "let's pretend." There is no need to act out the events physically, although you certainly could if you wanted to. What are you doing, what do you see, how are you feeling? How do you feel about your sister, and about Jesus' response to your request for assistance? Time limits are not important in this exercise, so for the next three or four minutes, enter into the experience of being Martha.

Enter the life of Martha now, before you read on.

Step Two: Mentally enter the life of another character.

Now try to get a sense of Mary's experience. Listen to Jesus. Imagine what he is saying that attracts you so. What do you feel about him? Who is he in your life? How do you respond to your sister's request? Are you feeling just a little guilty, or are you so captivated by Jesus that all other feelings and thoughts are excluded? Spend three or four minutes in Mary's sandals.

Enter the life of Mary now, before you read on.

Continue in this manner for as long as you like, "becoming" different characters each time. There is no rule against men imagining themselves as women or women entering the roles of men, nor any reason that we cannot enter into Jesus' human experience as well—be Jesus if you like. You can even make up an imaginary character, perhaps someone watching the entire exchange, and take that person's point of view for a while. Continue this until you feel a sense of being finished, of having completed this component of the exercise.

Step Three: Apply the story to your life.

The story is now real for you, not just intellectually or by faith, but through emotional resonance as well. It is part of your personal repertoire of imagination and memory.

It's time to stop the role-playing and look at the story's meaning for your life.

It may be harder for you this time around to sort out the Martha and Mary elements to your satisfaction. Like Martha, you may well "worry and fret about so many things." You are a person with responsibilities, jobs to get done. And yet we want and need space for God in life, for quiet reflection and prayer; the Mary side of life is necessary as well. With the story fresh in memory, reflect on its implications for your daily life. What do you do during the day? How do you feel about your schedule? Allow your feelings to come to the surface. Do you harbor Martha-like resentments? Do Mary-like longings arise? What is Jesus saying in your life today? Perhaps you can picture him speaking.

Allow four or five minutes for this reflection. New insights may emerge, and possibilities for change may be evident. Resolutions may result, or new tensions may be created. Follow them wherever they lead.

Reflect on the Martha and Mary sides of your own life now, before you read on.

This exercise is relatively simple, and can also be fun. It activates the religious imagination and involves the reader in the creation of the gospel message. Remember that, like the novel, the gospel message is re-created each time it is attentively read or heard.

Meditation can give the reader a new viewpoint on even the most familiar passages from Scripture. We have all heard the parable of the Good Samaritan scores of times, and most of us have heard dozens of sermons on its simple virtues. The road to Jericho is well travelled. Let the meditation take you past the preconceptions of what the parable is "really about" to allow a new reconstruction of its message in your own heart.

Exercise 3 in Scripture Meditation: The Good Samaritan

> But the man was anxious to justify himself, and said to Jesus, "And who is my neighbor?" Jesus replied, "A man was on his way down from Jerusalem to Jericho and fell into the hands of brigands; they took all he had, beat him and then made off, leaving him half dead. Now a priest happened to be travelling down the same road, but when he saw the man, he passed by on the other side. In the same way a Levite who came to the place saw him, and passed by on the other side. But a Samaritan traveller who came upon him was moved with compassion when he saw him. He went up and bandaged his wounds, pouring oil and wine on them. He then lifted him onto his own mount, carried him to the inn and looked after him. Next day, he took out two denarii and handed them to the innkeeper. 'Look after him,' he said, 'and on my way back I will make good any extra expense you have.' Which of these three, do you think, proved himself a neighbor to the man who fell into the brigand's hands?" "The one who

took pity on him," he replied. Jesus said to him, "Go, and do the same yourself." (Luke 10:29–37)

Step One: Mentally enter the life of one of the characters in the story.

Who will you be first? The traveller? The Samaritan? The man who sought to justify himself? Select one to begin your meditation, and enter the role for three or four minutes.

Step Two: Mentally enter the life of another character.

Let yourself become another participant or observer; see how things look from this new perspective. Continue this mental role-playing with additional characters until you feel you've finished.

Step Three: Apply the story to your life.

Take a few minutes for reflection. What new creation has appeared in your mind? What new insight? How does the Gospel speak to your life through this incident? Reflect on the newly emerging message of this familiar parable. You may or may not have come up with a marvelously original understanding, one that would be published in a Christian magazine. But you have certainly created a new, fuller understanding of what the parable means to you—and that's the point of the exercise.

Like the prayer of silence, this exercise takes a block of undistracted time. However, it can be profitably done on an occasional basis, while on the contrary, the prayer of silence needs to be done daily. Scripture meditation can become a powerful part of your prayer life if you commit to do it regularly even once or twice a week.

Exercise 4 in Scripture Meditation: Thinking about the Scripture Meditation in Your Life

As with the prayer of silence, some important questions need to be answered. Use paper and pencil in thinking about these issues.

- Does the Scripture meditation appeal to you? If you find this exercise immediately appealing, now is the time to make a plan. If, on the other hand, it felt clumsy and foreign, perhaps trying it a few more times over the next week will help you get comfortable with it. If it still does not fit you, spend your energy on something else. We do not all need to have the same personal rule of life.
- Can you really set aside twenty minutes for the meditation at least once or twice each week? If you cannot, be honest with yourself about that.

Do not read on until you have answered the two questions above.

If your answer to both questions is yes, now is the time to write a personal rule of life to make the Scripture meditation a regular stop on your spiritual journey. Identify one or two regular events in your week, and commit yourself to twenty minutes with the Scriptures *before* your automatic behavior. Be sure to write the rule down. The ink will last longer than your memory, and the written rule will endure beyond your good intentions.

9 · Brief Exercises in Family Prayer

Ordinary human life is bound up in the family. It may be possible to go through life without ever being involved in a family, but it is difficult for most of us even to imagine how such a thing might occur. Some people, of course, do choose to live alone, or in community with people who are other than literally their kindred. However, for most of us, life centers on the family into which we are born, grow up, and spend the majority of our adult lives.

God entered humanity through a family in Bethlehem. Before then, He had certainly found other ways to communicate with us. God spoke to Moses from within the burning bush, to Jacob in a dream, and to King Belshazzar through writing on the wall. But God also chose to dwell in the center of our lives, and His point of entry was a family. Jesus might have come to earth on a cloud, appearing in the form of an angel—but he took the form of a child, and grew up in a family.

The possibilities for love and acceptance are great in family life, as are the possibilities for frustration and rejection. Jesus must have experienced both extremes. He was raised in a loving environment, as shown by Mary's words of concern when, after three days of frantic searching, the twelve-year-old Jesus was found in the temple

(Luke 2:48). He was also rejected by his family, as shown by their refusal to believe his teaching (Mark 6:4), and by his own words: "Foxes have holes and the birds of the air have nests, but the Son of Man has nowhere to lay his head" (Matthew 8:20). Through shared prayer we can open our own families to Jesus. If we wish to live Christian lives and we live in families, our family relationships must be lifted up to God and lived out in His grace.

Exercise 1 in Family Prayer: Inventorying Family Prayer

With paper and pencil, review the moments of shared prayer that now regularly occur in your family. Do you pray together before meals or at bedtime? With whom do you pray? Are there times when praying together feels comfortable, a natural part of your routine? Shared prayer may occur several times each day, or only in grace before holiday meals. Making a list of your regular times of shared prayer will help in evaluating the current state of your family prayer life.

Make a list of regular times of shared prayer in your family now, before reading on.

Shared prayer may be common in your family, or it may be an unusual event. The inventory of family prayer is a good indicator of the importance of religion in the family. A family of serious baseball fans does more than go to an occasional game together; its members talk about the games, discuss trades, and study the box scores in the sports page. Similarly, the religious family does not limit shared prayer to Sunday worship. The care and concern given to God pours out into family life and becomes a part of the matrix of family communication.

We are all busy. Given our hectic lives, it can seem

that there is hardly even time to talk to the people we love most, the people with the greatest importance in our lives. Among all of our activities, we need to find some time for the people who most deeply matter to us, our families. And if we are serious about our faith, we need to find time to share that faith with each other at home.

Family patterns vary. In Jesus' time the family included an entire clan, and the word used for "brother" included cousins and other relatives as well. The line around the family was not tightly drawn. Forty years ago in the United States the word *family* generally suggested a nuclear unit of two parents, their children, and sometimes a grand-parent or two. Now the patterns vary widely. Often there is only one adult in a family, while many households fit the "nuclear family" model. Some couples choose not to have children, and others live in extended families where kith and kin blend together.

As we present family exercises, you're likely to en-counter some that do not fit your particular family. Single parents cannot do couple activities, and families without children cannot do the child-centered exercises. As you read, please do not feel that one pattern or another is presented as an ideal. Whatever your family situation may be, shared prayer and reflection can help open the door for Christ's entry.

Even with high divorce rates and the growing popularity of unmarried cohabitation, most families are based on a married couple. Even after the searing pain of divorce, most people find new partners and marry again. This bond of love and commitment between a man and a woman is the bedrock of the family. For most of us, marriage is the central commitment of adult life. The quality of that re-lationship sets the tone for our individual lives and for all other relationships within our families. Serious observers of human relationships, from psychotherapists to hair-dressers, note that every other part of a married person's life is profoundly affected by the state of the marital relationship. The strength of the couple as well as the depth of the individual prayer life can be greatly enhanced by sharing prayer.

Again and again, the Scriptures use marriage as an analogy for God's relationship to His people. One basis for this comparison is the shared intimacy of marriage, which is similar to the intimate relationship between God and mankind. When two people fall in love, they begin sharing secrets. Each wishes to know all that can be known about the other, and in return, each hopes to be known, accepted, and loved. Sexual intimacy in marriage expresses and extends this desire to know and be known. The goal of the spiritual life is to know God and to be known by Him—not God as an intellectual abstraction, but God as a warm, loving presence. Saint Augustine put it well in his classic fourth-century prayer, "Let me know myself, let me know you." Through Christ, God offers us the opportunity for such intimacy with Him. Like a spouse, Jesus enters our lives and knows our secrets. He shares our concerns, and experiences our sorrow and our joy.

People do all sorts of things to avoid the loneliness pervading much of modern life. Sexual promiscuity, frantically busy activity, alcohol and drug abuse are all common ways to escape being alone. Over the long term there are only a few solutions that work, providing more than temporary relief from the pain of solitary life. One is the shared experience that grows through a long-term committed relationship, especially marriage. Another opportunity is spiritual unity with God.

A number of Christian writers have spoken of spousal prayer, a form of prayer in which one relates to God as to a spouse, sharing the secrets of life. In spousal prayer, as in the relationship of marriage, you make yourself open to another, to one who comes into and shares your life. The married Christian has the unique opportunity to experience both kinds of sharing. The task is not simple, and the challenges are many—but the potential benefits are boundless.

Exercise 2 in Family Prayer: What Do You Know About Your Spouse's Spiritual Life? What Does Your Spouse Know About Yours?

You can do this exercise alone or as a couple. Done alone, it is a good review of your own perception of the level of spiritual sharing in your marriage. Done together, the exercise may open the doors of communication about prayer and other spiritual issues. However, you need to set aside enough time to share your answers and talk about the issues that the exercise raises. Allow at least an hour to do this exercise together.

Write down your answers to each of the following questions. If you are doing the exercise together, answer *all* the questions before you share your answers with each other. No peeking allowed! If you are doing the exercise alone, simply write your answers before reading on.

1. What are the important elements of your own spiritual life?
2. In what areas would you like to strengthen your spiritual life?
3. What do you believe are the important elements of your spouse's spiritual life?
4. In what areas do you think your spouse would like to strengthen his or her spiritual life?
5. How much do you think your spouse knows about your spiritual life?
6. Are you satisfied with the amount of shared prayer and other spiritual activity in your marriage?
7. Do you think your spouse is satisfied with the amount of sharing in this area?

8. In what ways, if any, would you like to increase sharing with your spouse about spiritual issues?
9. How do you think your spouse would feel about such sharing?

If you are doing this exercise alone, write down your answers to the questions before you proceed. If you would like to do it with your spouse, arrange for time to do the exercise together before you read on.

If you completed this exercise together, both of you may be interested in increasing shared prayer. Your answers to the questions may provide direction in how to proceed. If you did the exercise alone but feel that your spouse might be open to communication in this area, perhaps you will decide to raise the topic. The problem of dealing with a spouse who does not share your faith or your interest in shared spiritual communication will be discussed later in this chapter.

A common problem with shared prayer is deciding *how* to start. Any of a number of simple exercises in shared prayer can be your first step toward increased sharing and spiritual communication. Even if you have prayed together for years, one or more of these exercises may help to bring about more sharing. In order to do the exercises consistently, you will want to write a personal rule of life for shared prayer. Modifications in the general form of the personal rule will be given later.

Exercise 3 in Family Prayer: Praying Together as a Couple

When you pray together, allot about ten minutes for the experience. Because of the need for two people to express themselves and then react to each other, shorter periods are not practical. Here are some ideas for shared exercises in prayer.

- Consider beginning with spontaneous spoken prayer. Share your concerns and your thanksgivings, lifting them up to God together. Talk with each other about your lives, and share experiences of God in your daily living. If you enjoy singing, you may even want to sing a hymn during your shared prayer.
- Some people find it hard to pray spontaneously, even with someone they love and trust. You may want to say a morning or evening prayer service together. Many denominations have special sets of prayers in their service books for couples or families. These brief devotions usually include various prayers and the recitation of psalms. You may find this a comfortable form of prayer. If you do not know what short services are available, ask your pastor for direction.
- Reading the Scriptures aloud to each other can be enriching. Perhaps you will want to share brief readings selected along the lines suggested in chapter 5. After the reading, express your responses to the passage. It may raise questions for further study or issues for discussion. On the other hand, it may evoke a strong emotion. Share whatever comes to mind.
- Books of daily reflections are widely available in any Christian bookstore. You and your spouse may gain a great deal from sharing one of these on a regular basis.
- Some people enjoy shared contemplative prayer (chapter 7) or shared Scripture meditation (chapter 8). Either of these exercises takes on a new dimension if done in the presence of a loved spouse. Even though you do not speak during the inward part of the exercise, your being together will alter the experience. You might want to talk about your reflections after the prayer or meditation.

Select any of the exercises given above, or make up one of your own. Be flexible and creative with each other. Often what is "just right" for one person will not be comfortable for another. Be willing to talk about other ways to pray together if none of these exercises is satisfactory to both of you.

Make the necessary modifications in your personal rule of life to accommodate shared prayer. It is often difficult for an individual to find time to pray alone, and it is at least twice as hard for two people to find time to pray together on a sustained basis—a great deal of cooperation is required. Finding time is easiest if you can identify an automatic behavior you both do, or that one of you does consistently when you are together. In most marriages where children are present, the only time when extended prayer is possible comes after the children have gone to bed. Be sure to write the rule down and sign it after checking to be certain that both of you understand it in the same way. Time spent clarifying misunderstandings at this point will save much difficulty down the road.

If one member of the couple takes responsibility for remembering when it is time for prayer, the other partner *must* agree not to grumble when reminded. There is always an element of mortification (discussed in chapter 10) in choosing to pray when there are other interesting things to do. The partner who remembers should not have to cajole the other into prayer. If one partner or the other consistently gripes or makes shared prayer a misery to be borne by the other, the exercise simply will not work. Instead of drawing the couple together, prayer will have become a wedge pushing them apart. In such a situation, both are better off focusing on individual prayer instead.

One's spouse may not share the same religious faith or place the same value on prayer. This can be a source of tension in the marriage, as can any other important value that is not shared. The religiously active partner must be careful not to drive his or her spouse farther from prayer, and farther from intimacy in the marriage. There are a number of steps that can help one present faith without being obnoxious.

Exercise 4 in Family Prayer: Sharing Faith with a Spouse Who Is Not Interested

These are not one-minute exercises. Rather, they are ideas that can be woven into your relationship, making your Christianity manifest within a potentially stressful situation.

First, recall that God calls different people in different ways and at different times in their lives. God called Moses, and Moses tried to beg off, urging God to choose his eloquent brother, Aaron, instead. Jeremiah the Prophet was called by God before his birth; the thief on the cross next to Jesus did not find faith until the hour of his death. Peter, James, and John were called from their fishing boats, and Mary Magdalene from a life of prostitution. God can reach us, wherever we are, whenever He finds we are prepared. Jesus ended the parable of the vineyard laborers with the words of the generous master:

> I choose to pay the last-comer as much as I pay you. Have I no right to do what I like with my own? Why be envious because I am generous? Thus the last will be first, and the first, last. (Matthew 20:15–16)

Try to recognize the difference between your spouse's situation and your own. Accept the reality that your spouse can hear God's call only in his or her own time; you cannot force the message home. You can probably berate someone who loves you into going to church or praying with you at home from time to time, but conversion of the heart can only be the individual's response to God's call. You cannot make that happen, no matter how fervently you may wish to do so.

93

Live your faith. The more fully you can develop your own prayer life, the more ably you can assist your spouse in finding God. Deep reflective faith is usually impressive, and often contagious. Let your actions be the witness to your faith. If faith has filled your life with love, if you follow Christ with a happy heart, the value of your faith will be obvious to someone who lives with you. If, on the other hand, your faith is only words, there will never be enough of them to convince someone who knows you well.

Words do have a place. If there are times when you are comfortable telling your spouse about your religious experiences, do so, but avoid saying or implying, "You ought to be like me." Such an approach is sure to draw a negative reaction. Try to share your experience in a way that does not suggest you see yourself as morally superior to your spouse, or on a higher plane of enlightenment.

If your spouse does not share a value for prayer, before you read on, think awhile about ways to live your faith as a witness.

Once children are born, almost everything changes. Life after childbirth is both a blessing and a challenge to the committed Christian. Every plan you ever had, every notion you ever got from books on children, every idea you had about how you wanted to lead your own life, goes up for grabs once the first child is born. Having children changes life in ways one simply cannot have imagined. Things eventually settle down, and usually family life will come to resemble its prechild state, but of course it is never again quite the same. Child-rearing is one of the richest of life's experiences. But it is still a challenge.

The religious experiences we had with our parents can set much of the tone for our entire spiritual life. This is not to say that your parents predetermined your prayer life, but you will experience your spiritual journey in the light of your early encounters with prayer.

Exercise 5 in Family Prayer: Remembering Family Prayer from Childhood

Was there prayer in your family when you were a child? Did you go to church together, or say prayers at dinner or bedtime? With whom did you pray?

Take a minute to recall moments of prayer from your childhood. Let the feelings associated with those memories surface as well. Was prayer in the family of your childhood a happy time of sharing, or was it an enforced activity, something done only because it was required? What other memories come to mind in connection with prayer?

Spend a minute thinking about your childhood memories of family prayer now, before you read on.

If prayer was an important part of family life when you were a child, it is likely that there is an easy familiarity about prayer in your life. Even if you leave off prayer for years at a time, when you come back to it, it will feel like home. If your father knelt to pray with you, you may have assumed his attitude of reverence and respect. If, on the other hand, your father stayed at home while you and your mother went to church, you may have experienced some confusion about the value of prayer.

In teaching your children about prayer, what you do speaks much more loudly than what you say. Most children have finely tuned antennae that pick up hypocrisy at three hundred yards. If you talk religion from time to time but do not live it, your children will learn that religion is just something that people talk about. Your first priority in teaching your children about prayer is to be certain that prayer is an important part of your own life. They will observe your behavior, and learn from it.

It is relatively easy to pray with children. In fact, the only prayers heard in many households are the simple prayers that parents recite together with their children—"Now I lay me down to sleep," "Bless us, O Lord, and these thy gifts"—the prayers trip easily enough off our tongues. But as with the words of the Sunday worship service, these prayers can become so familiar that their simple profundity is lost.

Exercise 6 in Family Prayer: Praying with Your Children

Pray with your children in such a way that their remembered experiences of family prayer will be positive ones. First, recognize the child's verbal limits. A four-year-old may or may not be able to memorize the Lord's Prayer—however, there is no way he or she can understand what it means. Simple prayers, written or expressed in language appropriate to the child, are best. Second, brief periods of prayer are most productive for children. It's virtually impossible for a child to pray for prolonged periods, and the more prayer (or food, or love) you try to *force* on a child, the more resistance you are likely to encounter when the child is old enough to give *you* a hard time.

Brief periods of simple prayer, shared with parents who take prayer seriously (and joyously), are the best way to guide a young child's spiritual development. The prayers can take many forms.

- The simple recitation of grace before meals or bedtime prayers can be quite important. As you pray aloud with the child, make it clear that you take the words of the prayer seriously, rather than giving a machine-gun recitation: *Godisgreat, Godisgood, letusthankhim-forourfood, pass the potatoes.* As soon as your children are old enough, talk about what the words of these

96

prayers mean. Ask questions. For example, the question "Why do we thank God for our food?" may open the five-year-old mind to new vistas of understanding.

- Add brief, spontaneous prayers to the old standards. For example, bedtime in your home may be sealed with "Jesus, tender shepherd, hear me." Bring in a moment of spontaneous prayer by asking your child to thank God for something special that happened during the day, or to ask God for help with some difficulty. Be sure to pray along with the child, sharing both your thanksgivings and concerns.

- You can read Bible passages out loud and discuss them with your children. For young children, Bible story-books make the information much more accessible by substituting appropriate vocabulary. Even your littler ones are likely to surprise you with their insights.

- Many excellent books translate the Scriptures into stories for children. These stories make excellent bed-time reading.

- Children enjoy coloring books and puzzles, and there are many of these with biblical themes. If parents and children do them together, they become opportunities for shared faith and prayer.

- Your children may be able to sit quietly, briefly, with you while you "think about God." This shared quiet can be an early contributor to successful meditative or contemplative prayer in later life.

- It is best to follow the custom of your particular congregation in deciding whether or not to bring children to Sunday services. If your young child comes with you, do not make the mistake of imagining that the child can sit and remain fascinated by the service without any attention from you. Expect to devote some of your attention to helping the child follow the service. Many denominations have special books that help children follow the service. You might even want to make such a book of your own. Gift shops offer

"Quiet Books" filled with silent activities to occupy the child. When the child is older, help him or her read along, pointing out the proper part of the page, and encouraging participation by your attentiveness. The child sitting on a pew with no assistance is bound to get into mischief and to find the service boring. Help your child enjoy shared worship.
- Children are attuned to holidays, and love the excitement of special events. The events of the church year provide excellent opportunities for prayer with children. Involve them in the special celebrations surrounding Christmas, Easter, and the other holidays. You may want to develop family prayer services to fit your own holiday customs. For example, small children are delighted by the idea of a birthday cake for Jesus, and can readily enter into prayers connected with such a celebration.

For older children, the exercises listed above may not be appropriate. Teenage children especially may be seeking ways to establish their own controls over their lives, and so may be in the process of rejecting some of their parent's values, including their religious values. They may no longer attend church. In such cases, it is often best to approach the child as one might a nonbelieving spouse, living (and thus demonstrating) the profound attractiveness of the Christian life. Dragging your reluctant teenage children to church will only strengthen their resolve to stop going as soon as they possibly can. Pray *for* your children, pray *with* your children, pray *around* your children—all are good and fine. But you cannot force your children to pray for themselves. Prayer is the gift of God, the response of the heart to his call. If you develop your own spiritual life and live as a committed Christian, it is quite likely that your children will drift back into the church after they pass through their period of rebellion.

We live our lives mostly in families, and our relationships with God have to be developed in the family context. We can be missionaries to our own homes, bringing the loving grace of God into our kitchens, living rooms, and bedrooms. Shared prayer can help assure that He who entered a family in Nazareth many years ago is able to enter our own families today. If you have a relationship with God, He will be wherever you are and will be a part of whatever you do. If attention to God is built into your activities in what is called the secular sphere of life, your relationship with Him will grow as a result. Nowhere in one's life is the opportunity greater for this growth than in the family.

10 · Mortification: Putting God's Will First

We seldom use the word *sin* anymore. Nowadays we say that people who "commit sins" are sick; they're showing signs of stress, or are unable to adjust to life, or are narcissistic. The word *sin* makes us nervous. It implies a value judgment that, in our desire to be tolerant and understanding, we would rather not make about any person or group. We may be able to acknowledge the sinfulness of monstrous evil—the extermination camps, infanticide, chemical warfare—but we are quite uncomfortable with the idea of personal sin in the lives of individual people. However, the doctrine of sin and repentance lies at the heart of Christian teaching. One cannot seriously hope for growth in the Spirit of Christ without addressing human weakness and sin.

Exercise 1 in Mortification: Thinking about Sins You Have Witnessed

Take a minute to recall some things you have seen other people do that you found clearly sinful. What was it about the acts that made them appear to be sins?

Spend a minute calling examples of sin to mind before you read on.

Did you find it hard to remember examples of sin, or to put your finger on exactly what it was about an act that made it sinful? Because we are so aware that there are many possible causes of any behavior, we tend to place the blame for misbehavior on social or psychological factors beyond any one person's control. It is also easy to neglect the role of the individual in structural sin: People may starve because of unfair patterns of food distribution, or be unable to vote because of social inequities. However, any such large pattern is made up of a myriad of individual actions, each contributing to the whole.

At the core of the Christian message is the belief that people are responsible for their choices and for their actions. Our decisions are complicated by social and emotional situations, and by established structures and patterns, but in the absence of severe mental disorder, our decisions are our responsibility.

There really is sin. Sin is a theological concept referring to one's relationship with God. Sin is a state of separation from God, resulting from one's own actions. This separation does not seem important to the person who no longer cares about God in his or her life, one who already lives in the "post-Christian era." But it is central to the committed Christian. From Genesis to Revelation, Scripture calls on us to reform our lives. The Gospel demands that we reject whatever comes between us and God. It does not tell us that the task will be easy, or accomplished without pain.

Exercise 2 in Mortification: Recognizing the Inevitability of Sin

Jesus states plainly that it is impossible for people to avoid sin, even if they carefully follow all the established laws. In a story retold in all three synoptic Gospels, drawn here from Mark (10:17–27), he addresses the inevitable failure of human efforts at perfection, and at the same time offers us hope.

He was setting out on a journey when a man ran up, knelt before him and put this question to him. "Good master, what must I do to inherit eternal life?" Jesus said to him, "Why do you call me good? No one is good but God alone. You know the commandments: You must not kill; You must not commit adultery; You must not steal; You must not bring false witness; You must not defraud; Honor your father and mother." And he said to him, "Master, I have kept all these from my earliest days." Jesus looked steadily at him and loved him, and he said, "There is one thing you lack. Go and sell everything you own and give the money to the poor, and you will have treasure in heaven; then come, follow me." But his face fell at these words and he went away sad, for he was a man of great wealth.

Jesus looked round and said to his disciples, "How hard it is for those who have riches to enter the kingdom of God!" The disciples were astounded by these words, but Jesus insisted, "My children," he said to them, "how hard it is to enter the kingdom of God! It is easier for a camel to pass through the eye of a needle than for a rich man to enter the kingdom of God." They were more astonished than ever. "In that case," they said to one another, "who shall be saved?" "For men," he said, "it is impossible, but not for God: because everything is possible for God."

Spend one minute reflecting on the implications of this story before you read on.

The man went away sad. Jesus looked into the petitioner's heart and saw the one thing he valued more than discipleship. The wealthy man was not evil or mad; he was used to being comfortable and was not ready to give up that comfort. Being wealthy is not evil, but rejecting the call of Christ can be its sinful result. The man loved his place in society more than he loved Jesus, and Jesus knew it.

The roots of sin grow deep in the human heart. It is traditional to list seven deadly sins: pride, lust, avarice, gluttony, envy, sloth, and anger. Others may be added, such as the love of power and the idolatrous pursuit of security. Each of these sins grows out of ordinary human desires, common wishes, and hopes.

Sexual love, for example, is necessary for human survival and is a central part of Christian marriage. However, lust takes over when one's own sexual pleasure is the primary goal, without concern for the needs, wants, and desires of the partner. Rape, pornography, child molestation, and prostitution are all evils that can grow from the same root.

Similarly, in any human society someone must accept leadership. However, the love of power and influence can become a dangerous force in human life. Soldiers kill each other on a daily basis all across the globe because of the political ambitions of a few people. The leaders of the superpowers stand face to face, ready to destroy each other and the rest of the world along with them, their mutual enmity based on shared fear of what the other would do with complete power.

The roots of sin are not in themselves evil; they are good and make life possible. They are part of the basic makeup of humanity. Sin arises when we want something more than we want to follow Jesus. Jesus told one man to stop clinging to his love of social position and comfort. To another he might have said, "You are too dependent on being admired. Stand up for the Gospel among unbelievers," or "You spend too much time and money choosing your clothes," or "Give up indulging your love of rich food—it is destroying your health and your energy." Most of us go on repeating acts that we know interfere with our relationship with God. We do not want to give them up, and we choose them over discipleship.

Exercise 3 in Mortification: Standing in the Gaze of Jesus

Imagine for one minute that you are the person in the Gospel story. You stand before Jesus, eager to be received. Jesus looks steadily at you, and loves you, and then says that before becoming his disciple you must give up a sin that you have carried close to your heart, a sin that now stands between you and God. Hear his words. What is he telling you? What do you need to change?

Spend one minute in the gaze of Jesus, reflecting on a sin you have been reluctant to give up.

The call of the Gospel is quite clear. We must turn away from sin—"turn around your insides" is a literal translation of the New Testament word for repentance. If we are serious about following Christ, we will be committed to a true rejection of sin. Secure in the mercy of Christ, we must strive to banish from our lives all that separates us from God. We give up our selfish wishes so that we may be filled with the love of God. Just as Jesus hunted out the wealthy man's love of comfort, we should strive to dig out our hidden reservations, the small or large sins we keep for ourselves.

All of this may sound harsh or foreign to contemporary ears, but the doctrine of sin and repentance is a central Christian teaching. In an era of easy ethics and bumper-sticker morality (PROSPERITY IS YOUR DIVINE RIGHT—or—IF IT FEELS GOOD AND IT DOESN'T HURT ANYBODY, GO FOR IT!!), the idea of struggling against sin seems odd, like something snatched out of a medieval passion play. However, "dying" to sin, saying "no" to it, is a necessary part of the Christian prayer life. In prayer we attempt to empty ourselves of all that is selfish so that God may take over our lives. Paradoxically, as we die to self and God becomes more prominent in our lives, we become more truly self-fulfilled. We must die to self-interest and to our cravings, and not merely wish to do so, or talk about it without acting. Mind and body, emotions and spirit are so closely related that any attempt to separate them is unrealistic and fails to do justice to the full human stature that is our potential. We cannot wish for God to take over the direction of our lives while we actively pursue objectives and goals that are clearly at odds with the gospel message.

Deep inside us all lie the ordinary desires that can develop into pride, anger, lust, larceny, envy, laziness, and self-indulgence. Not even the saints have eliminated these roots. We can never be perfect, entirely free from the wish to have things our own way, but we can prevent our small sins from growing into a mat of weeds that would choke out the spiritual life altogether. The effort requires constant pruning of new growth from the old roots.

Christian teaching gives us a most effective tool for this task, traditionally called mortification—literally, "to make dead." Through mortification we take action against the ever burgeoning roots of sin by acting contrary to the underlying tendency. It should be noted that the concept of mortification is not the sole property of Christian spirituality. This idea, or one very much like it, is found in any spiritual discipline worthy of that label. There is a worldwide spiritual consensus: If you wish to see God, first get yourself out of the way.

Outside a spiritual context, mortification does not make any sense; set in the current ethos of "looking out for number one," it can appear downright insane. The basic tactic of mortification is to refrain from doing something that one wants very much to do. Mortification entails direct restraints on cravings for power, sex, money, comfort, food, and possessions. In fact, it restrains anything that we want more than we want to fulfill the will of God. There is nothing inherently evil in any of these desires. The problem is that the desire for any or all of them can easily begin to grow and run wild, consuming our energies and interests, turning our attention from following Jesus. Mortification keeps them in check.

Exercise 4 in Mortification: Reviewing Your Own Tendencies toward Sin

There are few things harder than recognizing one's own fallibilities. Anyone who has ever completed a high school or undergraduate course in psychology has become familiar with a long list of defense mechanisms—the mind's tricks to avoid thinking unpleasant thoughts about oneself. Our capacity to neglect our own flaws seems almost limitless. In this area, perhaps more than any other, it is immensely helpful to have spiritual direction or guidance from someone you trust who is also an experienced traveller on the spiritual path. The following exercises are given as an introduction to the process. You may wisely decide to seek additional assistance from your pastor, or from a spiritual friend.

Write a list of your own sinful tendencies, the strong wants and wishes that can push God into the background of your life. Begin each item on the list with the word *I*. Then write down what you think is the *central* tendency that may be the root of your sin; then an example of a sin that has sprouted from that particular root. Your list might look like this.

- I like people to think I'm sexually attractive, so I flirt with married men, and sometimes I let them think I might be available—just for fun.
- I want to be rich, and I invest every dime I can lay my hands on. I haven't given anything to a charity in years.
- I like to gamble. I can afford it, but last year I blew two thousand dollars that I could have used for better purposes.

106

- I like to take risks when I drive. Last week I nearly ran into a car full of teenagers when I came around the corner.
- I want people to like me, so sometimes I go along with things that I don't really approve of—just so I won't look odd.
- I like to be in charge. Last week at a meeting I didn't let anybody else get an idea in, just so the decision would be all mine.
- I need to get credit for things. I was on a church education committee and my name was left off the list in the bulletin. I really went into a rage.

Take time now to make your own list, before you read on.

You may not find a violation of one of the Ten Commandments in any of the behaviors you recall, even if there is a secret list of sins you decided not to write down for fear that someone might uncover it. Committed Christians often find it fairly easy to avoid big sins like killing people or selling addictive drugs; most of us are not even tempted in such directions. Our problems are more commonly caused by the pernicious little sins that populate our lives. These little "sinlets" may not seem like important issues. However, the ability to grow in prayer and in the spiritual life is directly related to the ability to rid one's life of petty sins. Whenever one does something *known to be wrong*, even if it is a very small act, the eyes must intentionally be turned away from God's presence. Perhaps, for example, one does not suffer frequent temptation to commit adultery, but destructive gossip is almost an everyday habit. Major transgressions can wake us up to problems in our lives, forcing us to confront them, but we can continue our small vices for years, twisting our

107

spiritual growth around a petty sin we have chosen to preserve.

When most people hear the word *mortification* they think of extreme acts, such as self-starvation, hair shirts, living in caves, and giving up sex forever. Most of us can thoroughly frustrate our own selfish wishes without going to extremes.

In fact, exhibitions of self-abnegation can backfire. One can mistake the practice of mortification for virtue itself, imagining oneself to be living on a higher plane of spiritual life than that occupied by other people. The resultant self-esteem rapidly degenerates into self-righteousness and spiritual pride. The desert fathers sadly noted that mortification tended to evolve into competitive piety, with each monk striving to be more humble than the next. In the southwestern United States a cult known as the Penitentes developed exaggerated forms of mortification such as beating the back with cactus thorns and voluntary crucifixion (using ropes rather than nails). The Catholic church wisely recognized the error in this behavior and banned the cult.

Mortification occurs whenever one chooses not to do an attractive but sinful act. The spiritual link is strengthened when one opts to replace a renounced undesirable behavior with a positive behavior.

There are sufficient ways to deny ourselves sinful gratification without leaving home.

Even a modicum of self-denial begins the process of mortification, especially when energy or resources are redirected from selfish pursuits to generous ones. For example, in doing any of the one-minute spiritual exercises, mortification is begun. One must choose prayer *before* the convenience of habit. Similarly, refraining from small but pleasurable acts known to be wrong is a powerful form of mortification. For example, a great deal of mortification would come about if people chose not to buy high-calorie snack foods and instead sent the money saved to programs for the world's millions of hungry refugees. Time spent passively watching football on TV could be spent playing catch with one's children.

There is some benefit in giving things up simply in order to gain practice in not having everything at your disposal. The venerable convention of sacrifice during Lent is an example of this approach. However, mortification is much more helpful if it is specific to personal needs. If Jesus had told the wealthy man to give up chocolate, the man might have returned to his mansion in a more contented state; but then Jesus would not have challenged him to examine his life. Mortification is most useful when it cuts right at the roots of one's most problematic sins.

Exercise 5 in Mortification: Designing Your Own Mortification

Return to your list of personal sins. Pick out one or two you would particularly dislike giving up. Those are the ones to go after.

Choose a form of mortification that will *directly frustrate* the sin in question. For example, to mortify a desire to take risks in your car, you might choose to obey the speed limit faithfully, *even when* you are in a hurry, *even when* you feel there is no chance of being caught and no discernible danger of an accident.

The underlying principle of mortification should be to choose virtue over vice; it is better—and often easier—to replace a petty sin with a positive act than to try to stop the sinning without having a replacement. Think about the sinful act, large or small, and then decide what you will do *instead*. Replace selfishness with generosity, laziness with effort, lust with respect. Often, a minute of prayer is an excellent way to mortify and block a selfish impulse. After a full minute of prayer, quite commonly one finds that the troublesome urge has become much easier to manage.

Going fifty-five miles per hour when you are sure you could safely whiz along at sixty-five may seem silly—unless you remind yourself why you are doing it. The immediate goal is to directly frustrate the desire to have your own way—to block your own tendency to sin. The ultimate goal is to open in yourself a space where God is free to take up residence. So as you carefully drive to work, remember that this is done, ultimately, for the greater glory of God.

Your personal tendency to sin may have to do with curiosity and gossip, and the chosen mortification may be to walk out on all such conversations or to make a point of saying something positive about the person being slandered. Not only does this mortify your own tendency to sin; it teaches others by example.

Your temptation may be to take credit for everything, and the mortification of that sin may involve going out of your way to be sure that others get their fair share of credit for work done cooperatively. You may be given to brag about your newest self-improvement campaign and choose to mortify that by not telling anybody that you are mortifying anything!

Your problem may be racism, which could be confronted by consistently looking for good in the people of other races encountered during your day.

Or you may have a tendency to overeat, which might best be mortified by giving up second helpings of your favorite foods. What is a petty mortification in one instance can be a potent spiritual prescription in another.

Whatever mortification is chosen, write the plan down. Be sure to include specific details of the positive behavior that you have chosen to replace your sinful actions. Then decide how long to continue this plan. Perhaps two weeks seems like long enough, or two months may be required. Make a commitment to sit down and review the effects of the mortification at the end of the selected period. It is especially important to look at the impact of mortification on your prayer life and on your experience with your other spiritual exercises. If the particular mortification has not been successful in diminishing the tendency to sin, choose another. Whenever performing mortification, be sure to recall that the point of the exercise is to diminish the power of one's own sinful tendencies in order to create a larger opening for God to enter.

Your list may take a form somewhat like this:

Tendency: I like to go out drinking to relax when I feel a lot of pressure in my job.
Resulting Sin: Lately I've been doing it several times each week, and I sense that I'm losing contact with my family.
Replacement chosen for mortification: I will make a point of going home and finding time to share my difficulties with my mate.
Time to evaluate this plan: Two weeks from now.

or

Tendency: I have a hard time handling criticism.
Resulting sin: I blame others for my mistakes. Recently some people at work have been in trouble because of things that were really my fault.
Replacement chosen for mortification: I will own up to my responsibilities. Whenever I am in the wrong, I will make that clear.
Time to evaluate this plan: This doesn't happen too often. I'll evaluate this plan in two months.

Write down a plan for mortification now, before you read on.

We are sinful people. We tend to want to do things our own way, in spite of the impact of those actions on others

111

or on our relationship with God. But we are also a re-deemed people. The forgiveness of our sins is already a fact, assured by Christ. We need only recognize and act upon our redemption for it to become a present reality in our lives. We shall never be sinless, but we are called to strive mightily to cut away at the roots of sin. God knows our weakness, and completes the work we can only feebly begin.

The horrible mess we have made of the world speaks to the terrifying depths of unchecked human selfishness. If we persistently choose respectful, generous actions over selfish, demeaning behavior, the world can become a safer, happier place for all of us. If we mortify our own wishes, God comes in to fill the empty spaces. Made truly whole by His presence, we can achieve good and decent lives.

"For men," he said, "it is impossible, but not for God: because everything is possible for God."

11 · The Others: Prayer and Christian Responsibility

Beware the false separation between spiritual growth and good works.

> If one of the brothers or one of the sisters is in need of clothes and has not enough food to live on, and one of you says to them, "I wish you well; keep yourself warm and eat plenty," without giving them these bare necessities of life, then what good is that? Faith is like that: If good works do not go with it, it is quite dead. (James 2:15–16)

If we become content to sit and pray, and do not put our hands to the labor of helping our brothers and sisters, prayer and Bible study become self glorification. We fill ourselves with good ideas, but nothing comes of them.

The clutter and pace of life make it difficult to find time for God—how much more difficult it is to find time for the poor. Given our major commitments to family, job, and social obligations, setting aside time for prayer might leave even less energy for the concerns of others. However, we observe that the opposite is true—prayer and good works go hand in hand. As sin grows from the roots of selfishness, sharing and responsible social action are the visible fruits of a sound spiritual life. There is a role for quiet lives devoted entirely to prayer and reflection, but busy Christians do not live in retreat from the world. We reside in homes and streets, and work in factories, schools, and offices. We must carry our spirituality into the struggles of men and women trying to create decent lives for themselves.

Exercise 1 in Christian Responsibility: An Inventory

Jesus made the expectation quite clear: Our final judgment is not based on the size of our bank accounts, how many friends we have, or the number of Bible verses we can recite from memory.

> Then the King will say to those on his right hand, "Come, you whom my Father has blessed, take for your heritage the kingdom prepared for you since the foundation of the world. For I was hungry and you gave me food; I was thirsty and you gave me drink; I was a stranger and you made me welcome; naked and you clothed me, sick and you visited me, in prison and you came to see me." Then the virtuous will say to him in reply, "Lord, when did we see you hungry and feed you; or thirsty and give you drink? When did we see you a stranger and make you welcome; naked and clothe you; sick or in prison and go to see you? And the King will answer, "I tell you solemnly, in so far as you did this to one of the least of these brothers of mine, you did it to me." (Matthew 25:34–40)

Take a minute to let this reading settle in, and then reflect on your recent past. Over the last three months, what have you done to answer this part of the gospel call?

Reflect on the passage and on your recent past now, before reading on.

Your inventory may have yielded a number of actions, large or small, taken on behalf of "the least of these brothers." Or did you find only a few acts of charity in your own life?

We tend to feel separated from the poor; from the old, the hungry, the sick, the mentally ill, and the victims of war or oppression. (Rather than repeatedly listing the many categories of human misfortune, we will generally refer to "the poor." Please understand that we use this term broadly, to refer to the wide spectrum of suffering humanity.)

In Christ's time, the poor and the rich physically encountered each other constantly. In contrast, most members of the American middle and upper classes are well insulated from poverty and injustice. Jesus told a story about a rich man at whose gate lay poor Lazarus, starving and covered with sores. The rich man had to step over Lazarus every day, just to leave his own house, and as he did so, he heard the poor man's pleas for aid and saw the sores on his body. We do not have the poor sleeping in our doorways; they live in other parts of town. By carefully choosing our routes, we need never pass through the poorer neighborhoods—or when we do, we're generally ensconced in a train, or in a car, the doors of which are likely to be locked.

We can avoid seeing the rest of the poor as well. The aged are in nursing homes. The retarded are in sheltered workshops. The severely mentally disturbed are settled into hospitals or nursing homes, or they live out of shopping bags, sleeping in downtown alleys. But they do not come into our neighborhoods, and we don't seek out theirs.

There are other forms of separation. By and large we have turned over the care of the poor to institutional charity and to government welfare programs. Often these do wonderful works of service. However, their existence permits us to shift aside the sense of personal responsibility expressed in the Gospel. If the Good Samaritan came across a man beaten by muggers today, he would probably go to a phone booth and call the paramedics, not giving his name for fear of lawsuit.

At that point, the larger systems of care-giving would take over. The man might be treated in a county hospital, get emergency relief from a United Way agency, be given temporary lodging at the Catholic Worker House, and partake of rehabilitation services through Lutheran charities. We have come to expect such reliable response from our organized charities. "The poor get food stamps—I help pay for them. What more do they need from me?" becomes a ready excuse for avoiding any personal action.

Finally, we tend to think of the poor and unfortunate as different than "us." This is easiest when there are obvious distinctions, such as race and language, but we can invent differences where no obvious ones exist. There is psychological trickery at work here. We naturally fear having bad things happen to us—nobody wants to be unemployed or hungry or sick and infirm. To diminish our anxiety, we need to believe that we are somehow protected, somehow not at risk. So we decide that a degree of fault lies with the people to whom bad things happen. We blame the victim, and thereby gain a false sense of security. However, this maneuver requires that we separate ourselves psychologically from the poor, increasing the already great distances between us.

This sort of separation breaks down during hard times. In a recession, even people with fine homes in good neighborhoods become unemployed. When "nice" people have economic problems, our trick of psychologically distancing ourselves from the unfortunate does not work so well, and we are left staring into the face of our own complacency and prejudice.

Exercise 2 in Christian Responsibility: Remembering the Faces of the Poor

Let yourself remember a specific time when you came face-to-face with poverty or sickness, with mental illness or

116

the loneliness of the infirm or aged. Recall a personal experience such as a visit to a nursing home or a community center in a ghetto. Perhaps you have lived in or visited another country, one in which the boundaries between the poor and the middle classes were not so tightly drawn. Or your life may bring you face to face with poverty every day; perhaps you or some of your friends are, or have been, victims of poverty.

Recall faces of the poor and the feelings you have experienced in looking into the eyes of these sisters and brothers.

When you have finished this, think of your experiences with the poor in the last three months. What boundaries now separate your life from the lives of the poor? What openings exist between your life and their lives?

Take a minute to think about the faces of the poor before you read on.

If we have the courage to look squarely into the face of human misery, our prayer and reflection on the Scripture will almost certainly produce a desire to take some action. But at the very point of thinking "I ought to do something," it is easy to be overwhelmed by the size of the problems. The poor are so many; so much of humanity suffers. What can a single, already very busy Christian do that would make a difference?

Mother Teresa is an unusual woman. She has chosen to live in the slums of Calcutta, caring for the very poorest of humanity's poor. All her time and her talents are devoted to this single cause. She has founded a flourishing religious order and has a global following that includes many people who contribute financially to her work. And yet scores of people still starve every day within blocks of her convent. Thousands of Calcutta's sick go untreated and many children are born, often into the briefest of lives, without the assistance of doctors or midwives. The human misery goes on. Why does she bother?

Jesus said that the poor would always be with us, and his call to us to meet their needs cannot be ignored. We are to do all that we can to improve the lives of the poor, though we know that we can never do enough. As Christians, we are to care about the least of his brothers. It is not to Mother Teresa's shame that people still starve; rather it is to her honor that some do not. Some receive care for their illnesses. Some have the opportunity to die hearing a comforting word, feeling a loving presence. Mother Teresa's work makes Calcutta a better city than it would be without her.

Each of us, by acts small or large, can make the world a better place to live in.

The Gospel is not fulfilled in the dutiful performance of good deeds. Its call goes deeper than this. Caring for the poor is a movement of the spirit. Clearly, mortification is involved whenever one acts with charity and generosity. As was pointed out earlier, mortification of one's own wishes can lead to spiritual growth.

But the call of the Gospel goes deeper still. To care for the poor is to be directly involved in Christ's own work. Acting on behalf of the poor, we place ourselves in tune with the movement of the Spirit. Like a boat with its sail open before the wind, this movement can give our lives new energy and direction. Acts on behalf of the poor are strengthened and multiplied when supported by a base of prayer and reflection, and the life of prayer gains new energy and vitality from acts of charity. By our giving, we enrich ourselves.

Exercise 3 in Christian Responsibility: Recalling a Small Act of Charity

Take one minute to remember a time when you went out

of your way to do something for a less fortunate person. Can you remember your feeling *after* the charitable act? How might such a feeling contribute to your own growth through prayer and reflection?

Take a minute to reflect on an act of charity before you read on.

Often an act of charity will give one a lift, a burst of spiritual energy. That energy, that sense of upward movement, can become part of your praying. Over time, an accumulation of those little lifts can elevate your entire life.

Most of us are not going to Calcutta to join Mother Teresa, nor can we give up our jobs to work full-time in the slums, nursing homes, prisons, or mental hospitals of our own cities. Some people *will* do these things, and it is to their great credit.

Most of us cannot or do not devote all of our lives to charity, but we can still make valuable contributions to Christ's work on behalf of the poor. Small acts of charity add up, and they add up in a number of ways.

The first way is obvious: Small actions accumulate into large ones. A rural hospital can be built with one donation of $100,000 or with ten thousand ten-dollar donations. The result is the same—the hospital is built.

Another form of accumulation is less obvious. People who are committed to work full-time on behalf of the poor can feel isolated and unsupported. Small acts of charity by people in other walks of life are immensely meaningful to those workers. Many people bring small donations of food to emergency food banks; they support and extend the work of those whose daily job is to try to fill the stomachs of the unemployed and the displaced.

Finally, as we've just shown in exercise 3, small acts of charity have a cumulative effect on the person making them. Even very simple acts, performed without fanfare, lead to the development of a charitable state of mind. This is profoundly enriching to the spiritual life.

Two basic ingredients go into the making of a charitable state of mind. The first is a mental receptiveness: One must recognize the call to action. The second involves setting oneself in motion, going to work on behalf of "the least of these brothers."

Exercise 4 in Christian Responsibility: You Are the Poor

It was noted earlier that those of us in the American middle class are separated from the poor. However, television, radio, and the newspapers bring us news each day of the disasters regularly befalling our fellow men and women. Unfortunately, the constant barrage has numbed us; we have learned to protect ourselves from empathetically experiencing their pain. The following exercise is designed to break down those mental barriers. It can be done in sixty seconds during a newscast.

Television news programs are designed with a single purpose in mind; that is, to assure that we do not turn the channel and miss the next commercial. To this end, news items are presented rapid-fire, one story ending with a lead that hooks us into the next. We are prevented from letting any single event sink in, because the pace of the program requires that we move on to new information— and new commercials. If the audience sat in a state of shock for too long, their distractedness might have a negative effect on sales of the products to be touted in the upcoming advertisements. So news programs do not dwell very long on any disturbing subject. This tactic may contribute to our apparent cultural ability to switch off our feelings. As the newscaster turns the page, we automatically stop worrying about the lady whose home burned to the ground and start thinking about the forthcoming bond issue.

It is possible to resist this profit-oriented form of conditioning. When you see a story on the news about some misfortune—the tale of a dislocated family, an interview with an unemployed factory worker, footage of people facing starvation in a time of famine—do not go along with the flow into the next, probably more upbeat, story. Instead, stop and think. Imagine for a minute what it would be like to be one of the people in the story. What if your home were blown apart by mortar fire? What if your son were starving? What if you had not worked in the last twenty-two months and had no job prospects? Let yourself enter the experience of the people you see on TV or read about in the papers. Use a watch to time yourself during this exercise. The tug of the next story is strong, and the habit of passively listening is well established. The imposition of the watch is an artifice that will help you make a clean break from the seductive rhythm of the newscast.

In doing this, you are likely to feel a great deal of tension, and perhaps frustration and helplessness as well. Let yourself become aware of these feelings. They are important feelings, because the people in the news story are also tense and frustrated, and may feel hopeless. Sharing their feelings in this way can help remove the barriers you have placed around yourself.

Breaking down the sense of distance between ourselves and the poor almost inevitably produces a desire to do something. But what? From both a practical and a spiritual point of view, doing anything, no matter how small, is vastly better than doing nothing at all. And, as has been noted earlier, small acts accumulate. But charity is not accomplished through good wishes—action must be taken.

Exercise 5 in Christian Responsibility: Brief Exercises in Charity

It is all too easy to feel overwhelmed by the size of the

problems. This feeling can lead to resignation, a fatalistic acceptance of things the way they are. "Wake up and face reality," we say to ourselves. But that really means "Give up and stop worrying." Nothing could be farther from the response Christ demands of us. For the person looking for a starting place, there are, as the following list suggests, innumerable small acts of charity that can be completely accomplished in a few minutes. They may not be as impressive as going to Africa to lead famine relief or organizing an inner-city food cooperative, but each of them permits you to add some small part to the accumulating acts of charity, the ongoing work of Christ.

- When you feel yourself touched by a story on a newscast, send two dollars to a charity involved in trying to make the situation better. (One dollar is not enough to cover the cost of processing your donation.)
- Take an hour to donate blood during a blood drive.
- Send a brightly-colored picture postcard to someone in a nursing home.
- Collect the old toys in your garage, and call the donation center to come pick them up during the annual pre-Christmas toy collection.
- Write a letter to a prisoner. Many newspapers carry requests for such correspondence in the "personal" ads.
- Call a coworker who has seemed down lately. Ask how he or she is feeling, and express your concern.
- Write to your representatives in Congress in support of food and agricultural aid in place of weapons shipments.
- Pull unused, unloved clothes out of your closet and drop them into the donation box on your way to work.
- Send a note to your county food stamp office, thanking the people who work there for their efforts.
- Pick up some extra items for a shut-in while you are out shopping.
- Call your local denominational charity. Ask the di-

122

rector what sorts of donations they may need at the present time. Then write a note for your church bulletin, informing people of the need; send the note to your congregation's secretary.

- Telephone a member of your city council and urge him or her to support making public buildings more accessible to the handicapped.
- Collect your old newspapers and drop them into a collection bin from which they will be recycled for charity.
- Drive a few minutes farther to eat at a minority-owned cafe, rather than eating at a fast-food restaurant owned by a multinational corporation.

This list can go on and on. It is limited only by your imagination and the opportunities in your life. Spend the next five minutes thinking about acts of charity that you could complete in a few minutes. Write the list down, and put it in your calendar. There it will serve as a reminder of your ability to do something more than accept the world as it is.

Spend five minutes listing brief acts of charity before reading on.

No five-minute act of charity is going to change the world, but it will help attune one's thinking to the poor and to the role of the Christian in assisting them. With each such act, the sense of personal powerlessness is diminished. Also, small acts foster larger acts. Beginning with small kindnesses, it is possible to find new openings, doors to a larger part in Christ's work of charity.

Perhaps the opening will be found in your own congregation. Most churches are involved in some form of organized charity, such as collecting money for the missions, or distributing groceries to the elderly. Some people find a chance to serve others as hospital volunteers, assisting at the Salvation Army or working with lonely children through the Big Brother and Big Sister programs. If you are fortunate enough to have the time to participate in such activities, it is highly likely that someone would be delighted to put you to work, for one hour or forty. Charity is not a matter of giving your money—it is an act of giving your life. More laborers are always needed in Christ's fields.

Jesus did not suggest that we care for the poor; he insisted upon it. Faith without good works is dead. As we seek spiritual growth, we must avoid the trap of self-centered personal development. The value of spiritual growth lies in knowing God and His will. There is no point in knowing God's will if we do not do it. Just as we are called to prayer, we are called forth from prayer into action: "Follow me."

12 · Evangelism: "Brother, Have You Been Saved?"

People freely share certain ideas and keep quiet about others. We readily discuss opinions about cars and schools, computers, and disposal diapers. We express opinions about consumer products quite directly: "I saved a lot of money when I got a..." "You simply must read..." "It would really be a mistake not to look at the new..." We are more careful with opinions about personal topics such as raising children or managing the household budget. If we fear being judged critical or out of line, we are even more likely to keep quiet. Finally, there are some things that one simply does not talk about in polite company. It is commonly understood that nice people do not share their opinions on sex, death, toilet habits—or religion.

Many of us cannot talk comfortably about religion. It is a very personal topic. We fear offending people or being obnoxious, shoving our beliefs on others. We would rather not be classified as pushy preachers, so we say nothing at all about religion. Now and then we may experience a twinge of unease, even guilt, about our silence, especially when we see others bold enough to stop people on the street and "speak up for Jesus." There is something admirable in being so public and straightforward about faith. But our hesitations leave most of us saying nothing at all.

Exercise 1 in Witnessing: The Divine Commission

Christ's final words to his disciples contain the Divine Commission. As you read this passage, think about the call it expresses.

> Go, therefore, make disciples of all the nations; baptise them in the name of the Father and of the Son and of the Holy Spirit, and teach them to observe all the commands I gave you. And know that I am with you always; yes, to the end of time. (Matthew 28:19–20)

What is Jesus saying to *you* in these words? Take a full minute to let the message settle in.

Before you read on, spend one minute thinking about how the Divine Commission applies to you.

Evangelism is an old word. It comes from the Greek word *evangelion*, "good news." Each Christian is commissioned to spread this Good News. Since the founding of the church, Christian men and women have spread the word that God calls us to a better life. There are many sorts of evangelists, and we carry different images of them in our minds. Some of us think of dedicated men and women going from door to door, offering pamphlets with a smile. Others recall pictures of priests in white habits spreading the Gospel in Africa or Asia. Still others call to mind inner-city preachers crying out to the crowds at busy bus stops, or travelling preachers at tent meetings. The message is usually the same. "Jesus is Lord. We must follow him and reform our lives." Styles of communication differ, but the message is the same across centuries and continents.

Faith is a gift from God, but the news that inspires it is usually delivered by a human messenger. Evangelism is part of the Christian life. When one has found something

126

that makes life better, it is only reasonable to let other people know about it. The Gospel is quite clear: It is our job to pass the word along. However, many of us hold back.

We excuse ourselves by thinking of evangelists as full-time workers, people who go to the missions to save pagan Africa or who spend their lives on the revival circuit. Since we are not able to leave our obligations to be full-time evangelists, we feel relieved of the responsibility. It is so hard to know what to do on a part-time basis—so we give a few dollars to the missions and let the professionals handle it. Further, many of us are uncomfortable with the very idea of accosting strangers on the street (or unsuspecting friends at dinner) with the questions, "Have you been saved?" "Have you accepted Jesus as your personal savior?" The direct and unsolicited intrusion practiced by some of the more aggressive Christians can be heavy-handed and even arrogant. This style of evangelism, especially common with television preachers, often carries the message that nobody is "saved" unless their religious experience and expression are exactly the same as those of the evangelist. Many of us would never evangelize in this way, but have no idea what else one might say.

Exercise 2 in Witnessing: Who Evangelized You?

The first and best teachers of our faith are often parents. Others may remember special teachers in catechism or Sunday school. Those who came into the church as adults can often name easily the people who led them to faith.

Yet many of us who grew up as Christians have watched our friends fall away from the church, generally sometime after their high school years. A child's faith and an adult's faith are not the same. In youth we all need models, full-grown Christians after whom we can pattern our adult actions and beliefs if we hope to negotiate the bridge to

127

mature Christianity. We are still Christians, at least in part, because of the men and women who showed us the value of grown-up Christianity. We may have met them in church, at work, or in school. They may have been full-time ministers, or bricklayers who shared their faith one day over lunch at a construction site. They may have gone out of their way to share the Good News, or just lived their lives in ways that showed the depth and value of their faith. Some were consciously acting as teachers, while others were unaware that we were learning from them. Intentionally or not, those people made Christ manifest in our lives. They announced the Good News. They evangelized us.

Take a minute and remember the men and women who helped shape your faith. These people were your personal evangelists, commissioned by Christ to bring the Good News to you. What did they say to you that made a difference? How did they share the Word with you?

Take a minute to remember the evangelists who have influenced you.

It is quite likely that at least some of the important people who come to mind were not full-time evangelists or religious instructors. Most evangelists are ordinary people who respond to Christ's urging to spread the Good News. We are called in many ways. Christ finds us where we are, and sends us evangelists who speak in language we can understand. As others spoke for Christ to us, we can speak to others for Christ. Just as there are many different styles of prayer and worship, there are many different ways to pass along the Gospel.

Busy people can be evangelists. People who feel pulled in many directions at the same time can be evangelists. People who have doubts and who dislike being preachy can be evangelists. Anyone who shares his or her faith becomes an evangelist.

Only busy Christians can be evangelists to the busy world—no one else is there to spread the message. The only people who can take the Gospel to banks, teachers' lounges, living rooms, boardrooms, or factories are busy Christians. If they—you—do not speak up, who will?

The importance of physical presence cannot be overstated. It is impossible for the word of God to go into a place unless a Christian enters carrying it. Moreover, the presence of a "real, live" believer communicates much more vividly than any pamphlet or book or radio sermon ever could. In Jesus, God becomes physically present and accessible. He is available in a way that sight, smell, hearing, touch, and even taste can grasp. His human body ate and slept, bled, died, and rose. In Jesus, our spiritual union with God becomes physical reality. The spirit of God speaks to us best through the physical body of Jesus.

The work of bringing humanity to God belongs to the Holy Spirit, speaking directly to the depths of the individual heart. As Jesus made God physically present to humankind, we make the Spirit physically present to one another. Anytime you let another person know about your faith, your presence becomes a reminder that God acts in human life. You become an evangelist.

Exercise 3 in Witnessing: Recalling Your Own Acts of Evangelism

Can you recall times when you spoke up about your faith? Perhaps you talked with a friend about your religious experience. You may have told someone at work that you were going to a church service that night after dinner. You may have turned down an invitation to play racquetball, explaining that you were going to church. Or you may have taken someone out to dinner with the express purpose (revealed in advance, ideally) of talking about your church.

Try to remember occasions when you have been an evangelist, when you were the physical presence of the church in the lives of other people

Spend a minute thinking about your own acts of evangelism before you read on.

Evangelism is a source of spiritual growth. Along with prayer and mortification, study of Scriptures, and care for the poor, it is one of the acts that both embodies and strengthens Christian life. Sharing our faith enhances it. As believers, we are rooted in the community of faith, the church. Apart from the church there can be no true Christian faith. When we invite others to consider the Good News, we become the embodiment of the church. The church is no longer a building or a nameless group of people. It takes on a human face, a human voice, and a human heart—yours. You are the church for the person whom you invite to Christ.

This is the sort of responsibility that makes thinking people tremble. Rightly or wrongly, people judge the value of Christianity by looking at individual Christians. Once we let people know about our faith, they begin to judge Jesus by looking at us.

It may be much easier to evangelize strangers on street corners than people we see day after day. Hand the passerby a leaflet, urge him to seek God in his life, and watch him walk away. The interaction ends there. The recipient of this sort of evangelism does not hang around to ask embarrassing questions. He might think you silly, or even shout obscenities, but he will not be there for the next six months, observing your behavior, looking for the reality or the absence of your faith. Preaching the Gospel to strangers requires only the ability to get over stage

130

fright. Evangelizing on television ("Praise God, and send the check today!") insures that your listeners will never become too inquisitive about your habits. However, exposing one's Christianity to the scrutiny of friends and coworkers takes courage and a willingness to live the Gospel rather than just talk about it.

Exercise 4 in Witnessing: Letting the Secret Out

One simple but powerful way to share your Christian faith is to mention it *when the subject is not expected.* Telling people about Jesus at a prayer meeting is important, but you will make more impact on people by casually mentioning faith at a business meeting. Testimony is part of the expected ritual at many church events, but it comes as a surprise in the office or at the PTA.

You probably will not want to launch into a sermon during a roll call vote at a club meeting, or collar people into prayer meetings in the cafeteria. That sort of behavior generally turns away more people than it attracts, and is almost certain to earn you the label "religious nut." However, mention church in passing, without elaboration, and people become aware that you are a Christian; you may be the only actively religious person in the room.

You can make others aware of your Christianity, simply and quietly, through comments that might be as simple as these examples.

- "I called John Sunday after we got home from church."
- "We're going on a picnic with the Parish Young Couples on Saturday."
- "I have to think about this question in a religious context. As a Christian, I feel it's my responsibility."
- "I will pray for you."

From that point on you are an evangelist to the people in your busy world. They know about your faith and will observe you in its light. Your every act will be evaluated: "This is what Christians are like."

Take a moment to think about some situations in which you interact with other people, whether encountered singly or in groups. Have you ever let out the secret of your Christianity? Do the other people even know that you go to church?

If there are situations where your faith is still an unknown quantity, how might you let people know? Are there opportunities to mention your church activities? Could you sneak the word *Christian* into a conversation? You might bring up your child's baptism, or mention someone you saw last night at a prayer meeting. It only takes a second or two to make the unknown known. Three or four words might be enough to begin your evangelism.

Once people know about your Christian faith, they will look at you differently. Right now, think how it might change things if the people at your job or school, or your friends at the gym, or in your mothers' group knew that you were a committed Christian. Would they react differently toward you? Would you want to relate to them in different ways, realizing that you had become the physical presence of the church in their lives?

Take sixty seconds now to consider the ways that letting out the secret would change your life.

Evangelism involves risks. Even if you are quite moderate in your approach to others, some people are going to think less of you because of your faith. Some think that all religious people are neurotic, or not very intelligent. But there are also people with big empty places in their hearts, and people who would like to become involved in church but do not know how. There are people in times of trial who only need to hear a few words of encouragement to open or reopen their lives to the Christian message. There is no way to know who is who until the words are spoken. Some people will want to stay as far as possible from anybody who mentions religion except to make jokes about it. Others may find a few words of faith, openly shared, to be the key that opens their hearts to change.

Letting the secret out is the first step, and in most situations there will be no more to do. For example, at a meeting with a group of strangers, mentioning church may be a powerful act of witness. Going on about the subject is likely to be seen as intrusive or irrelevant, and so there may never be an opportunity to say more. On the other hand, someone at work or school may express an interest in your comments about religion, and there may be opportunities to follow up tactfully with these people.

At this point, some Christians get quite heavy-handed. It is almost a joke that when certain people get started, they never quit, whether or not their overtures are welcome. A friend and his wife once went to dinner at the home of a couple and were asked if they would like to see "some movies" after dinner. The movies turned out to be dogmatic religious films, attacking the very church that the innocent visitors regularly attended. These were followed by a strident recruiting talk, which ended only when the guests finally asked for their coats and left. Inevitably, most people resent such a barrage.

Religion cannot be sold with the same tactics used to peddle swamp real estate. If someone makes it clear that more information would be welcome, it is time to open up, sharing personal experiences, offering to get together and talk, or even inviting the seeker to come to church. The critical issue is sensitivity. Especially in the beginning, it may be more important to listen to the other's religious experience than to share your own. Respectful evangelism ought to be the sharing of religious journeys, rather than one-way salesmanship. If someone seems interested and comfortable discussing religion, then talk. However, pushing people along faster than they want to go is an act of insensitive arrogance. Many people have had very negative experiences with aggressive Christians, and they pull away as soon as the "Win-a-Soul-for-Jesus" push is detected. It is hard to blame them.

Exercise 5 in Witnessing: Comforts and Discomforts

Try to imagine that you are someone who does not go to church—that you never were a church member, or that you dropped out a long time ago. Now, think about what it would be like to have someone talk with you about Christianity. What sort of tactics would make you nervous or uncomfortable? What sort of approach would help you feel more at ease? What words or actions would feel like an invitation rather than an assault? Give yourself a minute to really consider the differences.

Before you read on, think about comforts and discomforts in being offered the invitation to Christianity.

There are no magic formulas for sharing the gospel message. It seems important to listen, and to avoid pressing religious opinions on people who do not want to hear them. And remember that abstract discourses—"The Church is a body of caring individuals who blend their hopes and aspirations and become thereby the Mystical Body of Christ"—say little to the neophyte looking into the church for the first time, or to the turned-off Christian contemplating a return to church. Instead, tell them what people do in your church, or how religion makes a difference in your life.

- "Last month our congregation raised a thousand dollars to pay the bail of a woman who was in jail because the government didn't recognize her as a war refugee."

- "On Mondays I pack groceries that get delivered to retired people. It gives me a feeling of helping out."
- "A man in our church was out of work, and the church members got together and hired him to do maintenance until he got his new job."
- "I pray for fifteen minutes every morning. It gives me a good start for the rest of the day."
- "I had never read the Bible until last year. I joined a Bible study group, and we worked our way through St. Paul's letters. There are really a lot of beautiful ideas in them."
- "I hadn't taken Christianity seriously at all until I met Howard. He really helped me see the importance of prayer. Maybe the three of us could have lunch sometime."

Perhaps your personal invitation could best be extended through one or two minutes of conversation about your own spiritual journey. Share news of what God has done for you, and what you are doing as a member of the church. Faith must be significant at the local level. If Christianity does not make a difference to individual lives—in this case, yours—it cannot be all that valuable. The clearest message may be, "This is what I'm up to as a Christian, and this is why Jesus is important to me."

Beyond this, evangelism is a matter of style. People are able to receive a message only when it comes in a language they understand. This is as true of the Good News as it is of any other information. The messenger is an important part of the message.

Christ calls us to be evangelists. As Christians, it is our job to tell other people about the Good News. Perhaps the hardest but most important sort of evangelism is sharing faith with the people around you. Busy Christians must carry the message to where the people are, which is in the busy world. Each of us is a member of the Body of Christ. Wherever we go, we are the physical presence of the church and of the Holy Spirit. With prayer and in faith, we have the opportunity to do our small part in the work of "baptizing all nations." Each of us can become a living invitation to follow Christ.

13 · When God's Answers Are Hard to Hear

Rhythms abound in life, and there are seasons in all things. There is no escaping the ebb and flow of human life; not even the spiritual life stands above its tides. There are times when all the flowers of prayer seem to bloom at the same time, when the sense of closeness to God is strong and comforting. It feels as though those good times will go on forever. God, after all, is eternal—why should the feeling ever change? But it does. Periods of spiritual drought are an undeniable part of the Christian life of prayer.

Feelings change because they are human feelings. God is eternal, but our enthusiasm is not. Emotions, convictions, feelings of love and hate, religious fervor, even the sense of God's closeness, are all the products of our own minds. God is not man's creation. God is an eternal, unchanging reality. However, the human response to that reality is the creation of the mind. On some walks through the woods we find ourselves almost intoxicated by their beauty; on other days we are so preoccupied by our own concerns that the same beauty evokes no response at all. The woodland has not changed, but our reaction to it is different. God does not change, but there are seasons in the spiritual life because of the changeability of the human condition.

Our level of excitement about any long-term project fluctuates. Any marriage lasting more than a few months has good and bad times. Some days we love our jobs; on other days, going to work feels like punishment for unrecalled sins. There are times when study is easy, when new ideas and information seem to flow into memory all by themselves—and other days, when nothing wants to stay in the mind for more than a few seconds. Everything is easy when enthusiasm and energy are high. On the "other" days, everything feels like work.

We are a nation of enthusiasm addicts. We tend to stick with a project only as long as the first burst of energy lasts, and start looking for a replacement as soon as we come down from the "newness high."

Consider the magical euphoria about the first few days or months of love. Time, familiarity, and fatigue eventually diminish the initial ardor. Mature, deeply loving relationships develop only after the first heady days have passed. However, many of us know people who go from relationship to relationship, breaking off as soon as the newness begins wearing thin. Addicted to the exhilaration of falling in love, those people never experience the fulfillment of long-term commitment.

Similarly, there are free-lance activists who go from political cause to political cause, always seeking the excitement of a new project. In our popular arts, we are slavish followers of fads, with new rock bands replacing old ones every few months, new movie stars replacing the old as rapidly as fan magazines can be printed. And we have fads in sports: One year tennis is the fashionable sport, the next year everyone is playing racquetball, and the third year finds us all lifting weights. We follow the excitement of the new because it is so much easier to ride the next wave of energy than to persist in anything after the euphoria has subsided.

We do the same thing in our spiritual lives. Americans hop from church to church, and even from faith to faith, almost as easily as they buy a new pair of fashionable shoes. Each revival meeting, each new parish priest, each new Eastern guru brings a breeze of fresh enthusiasm. The new spiritual project seems like the answer, the sure solution to all of the old problems. But just as surely as the winds change, the rush of newness is certain to reverse itself. If religious commitment fades with the passing of the first enthusiasm, one is right back at the starting line. All the old resentments and doubts and questions come back. Spiritual growth takes time and persistence.

Exercise 1 in Persistence: The Parable of the Sower

This is what Jesus told a large crowd of people who were excited about hearing the new teacher.

> "A sower went out to sow his seed. As he sowed, some fell on the edge of the path and was trampled on; and the birds of the air ate it up. Some seed fell on rock, and when it came up it withered away, having no moisture. Some seed fell amongst thorns and the thorns grew with it and choked it. And some seed fell into rich soil and grew and produced its crop a hundredfold." Saying this, he cried, "Listen, anyone who has ears to hear." (Luke 8:5–8)

Can you recall some times when your spiritual life has suffered the fate of the seed that fell on rock, growing up quickly, and perishing just as quickly? Maybe you disliked the church you were attending, and made a change. At first the new congregation seemed perfect, but eventually you became aware that it had its own flaws. Or you might have heard an exciting speaker and been filled with excitement and good resolutions, which faded after a few days.

Take a minute to remember times of fading, flagging enthusiasm before reading on.

A cynic once told an evangelist that "being saved" must be a worthless experience because so many people went back to their sinful ways after accepting the Lord at a revival meeting. The evangelist pointed out that being saved was like taking a bath: Being clean once did not prevent getting dirty again. This remark contains a profound truth. Christian commitment is not a matter of a burst of enthusiasm. One is not "saved" on the days when energy is high, and "lost" again when the spiritual high has faded temporarily. The real danger lies in turning away from Christianity when things get difficult.

There will always be some new fad, some new formula for solving all of life's problems. However, true depth comes from following the same spiritual path over months and years. One must persist through the inevitable crests and troughs in the waves of enthusiasm. Anyone can follow Jesus in Galilee, when things are going well and everybody loves the new healer in town. The crowds drop away on the way to Calvary. We want easy solutions and we want them right away—and when they are not forthcoming, it's easy to decide that there is something wrong with God.

Sooner or later, low periods are sure to come. Prayer will not "do a thing for" you. You won't "get anything out of" going to church. Being a Christian will no longer be as "fulfilling." This is a very distressing situation, especially for the person who takes faith seriously.

Developing a personal rule of life and beginning regular Scripture reading can bring about a sense of closeness to God. But the rent still needs to be paid. Children still get sick. And on some days, reading the Bible will feel like doing homework. If one has become accustomed to getting good feelings from spiritual activities, responses of pain and loss will surface when the zest and emotional lift are missing. Instead of the accustomed inspiration, one experiences a flatness of feeling, a dryness. One goes through the steps of prayer, but prayer seems like an empty act— like what Jesus called "vain repetition." Going to church comes to feel like a charade. All the good reasons not to bother with any of it come back to mind. There is no longer joy and emotional satisfaction in meditation, liturgy, or prayer. Using the imagination or trying to rekindle emotions may or may not lift the malaise. The intention to pray remains, but the ability to do so seems to have disappeared.

If the trough of the wave is deep enough, it will bring up troubling doubts about faith. During periods of dryness, prayer can seem dreadfully boring and pointless. God seems distant, and He had seemed so close before. It is easy to start questioning his very existence. The idea of giving up the entire endeavor will arise, and one may start to feel foolish for ever having gotten involved with God at all— besides which, there is always the attractive possibility that some new enthusiasm will carry one off for a while. "Why endure all this misery when Master Kim or Sister Sarah offers the promise of a quick fix for your spiritual woes?" This is what Christian tradition has called the dark night of the soul. It seems that God is dead. The Gospel appears to be a cruel joke. The Christian who has taken religion seriously will probably experience some real depression during these periods. The joy of spiritual gifts is so great that their absence is painful. Jesus had seemed so near, his comforts had been so sure, and now one feels alone again. Giving up can seem like the only reasonable thing to do. Go work in the garden or read a book about household finance—at least you can get some practical use out of it—or take up golf. One was silly to believe that God cared at all. It's easier just to forget the whole thing.

This is an old and familiar situation. The teachers of the church have long said that there is no true faith without temptation. Lost enthusiasm is the natural course of events, and only from the depths of dryness can mature faith grow. In such times we experience the cross of Christ in our personal lives, and in our prayers. Jesus told us that we would walk in the way of the cross, and that "the servant is not greater than the master." He said so over and over, but we do not want to hear this message. We want to remake God in our own image, to have Him be the guarantor of our success and personal fulfillment. We want a God who gives us prosperity and happiness. We want a God who makes sure that we have nice things, who will kiss our hurts and make them well. That God is as surely an idol as was the golden calf. Jesus promises us the cross. He promises that people will reject us because of him. He tells us that our idea of comfort is a hoax that will just get in our way.

This promise is not a lie, and when he keeps it, we want to turn away. We forget that the resurrection can come only after crucifixion.

We want God to come to us bringing only joy and comfort, but at times He chooses to come to us in our darkest hours. God revealed Himself to the Hebrew people in the midst of their suffering and slavery. He delivered them, but their deliverance was completed only after years of wandering. Christ came to us in a stable, born in the midst of poverty. He lived his life amid the suffering and the poor. He ended in his "hour," his final and greatest moment, giving up his life in dreadful suffering and agony. Even he cried out on the cross: "My God, my God, why have you forsaken me?" No Christian can escape the personal implications of following a God who reveals Himself in this way. This is not a God who promises to make life painless. The apostles did not want Jesus to accept the cross; they wanted a deliverer who would free them from the Romans. They consistently misunderstood his purpose throughout his public ministry.

We still want Jesus to make everything better, to make things turn out our way. He would not do it for his disciples, and he will not do it for us.

Times of aridity can be times of profound growth in

faith. We all begin our spiritual lives worshiping false gods, gods whom we can contain in our small minds and our small understandings. The human mind can no more contain God than a kite can contain the wind. As we grow in spiritual knowledge and maturity, our false gods must crumble. As our self-created idols fall apart, we feel abandoned, left alone—we think that God has forsaken us, or worse, that He never existed. But until the false gods are cleared away, there is no room for the One Who Is.

During periods of dryness, it seems that the God we believed in is not there. He is not. He never was. But, without the experience of dryness, there is no chance to find out that one has been worshiping idols. God exists, but we need to remove our idols before we can see Him. As long as things go along fine with our misconceptions, there is no chance to learn the truth. The key is persistence. Pray the Our Father ten thousand times, and it can come to seem a leaden task. Then, all of a sudden one's eyes and ears are opened to what it really means to say "our Father" and believe it. The hours of boredom and dryness prepared the mind for the new understanding. It seems that only when we have burst beyond the limits of old understandings can we come to new ones. Only when we have lived through the death of our false gods and our false hopes and have stopped trying to rewrite the Gospel from our own tiny human perspective can we die and rise again with Jesus.

The apostles were transformed by the presence of the risen Lord, and we too must become open to his transforming presence. Nobody knows what really happened to the apostles in their encounters with Jesus, but it is clear that they emerged as different people. Once they understood the meaning of Christ's death, they were finally able to experience his peace. They went out and faced everything that the Roman Empire could throw up against them.

Periods of dryness come before new visions and new growth. During times of lost enthusiasm it is hard to believe that one is being transformed into a better Christian. The sadness and the dissatisfaction are inevitable by-products of the death of false beliefs. Beyond the darkness lies the light of the presence of God, without false images blocking our view. But the dryness must be endured. Like the ancient Hebrews, we must come through the desert. We have to let our idols die, and give up on everything we have *wanted* God to be so that we can discover Him as He really *is*.

The Christian faith assures us that there will be a positive outcome, that the period of aridity will be followed by a blossoming of trust and consolation. Unfortunately, it is very difficult to believe that when one is at the bottom of the trough. If spiritual growth were a multiple-choice test, it would be simple to mark answer C: "Greatly enhanced faith will return to those who persist in devotion and prayer." However, knowing the correct answer and successfully living through the experience are two very different things. It is hard to pray during periods of dryness precisely because at those times prayer seems like a useless thing to do.

Exercise 2 in Persistence: Getting Through the Hard Times

You may or may not have confronted the dark night of the soul. However, all of us have had periods of lost enthusiasm. Perhaps you can recall a time when you felt a loss of enthusiasm, a loss of energy for your faith. How did you get through that period? What helped you persist in your prayer?

Before you read on, spend a minute recalling a time when faith was difficult.

144

There is no cut-and-dried formula for coming through this sort of experience. Renewal of faith, like the Resurrection, is God's act, not ours. There is no way to hurry the process along. However, there are some suggestions that may be helpful to the Christian being tried by periods of spiritual emptiness.

First, remember that your experience is not unique. It is a predictable part of spiritual life, rather than a sign of craziness or of a particularly sinful nature. This knowledge may not reduce the pain, but it may render it more understandable and perhaps less frightening.

Second, it is critical to stay involved in the activities of faith, even when they feel wooden or artificial. Continue attending church and studying the Scriptures; they are powerful means of grace. The rhythm and fellowship of church life can support you when your personal energy is low. It is particularly important to resist the temptation to escape by leaving the church or abandoning your Christian spiritual exercises. This is not the time to take up Zen or join a new movement: Escape is tempting, but it will prevent the growth that persistence brings. Just as it is possible to have a series of love affairs and never a marriage, one can go from spiritual path to spiritual path and never develop any depth.

Third, this is a time to seek spiritual support and guidance. Your pastor may be an important source of guidance. If you have never had a "spiritual director," now would be a good time to find someone who can understand and help. Contact with other believers can be critical in coming through periods of dryness, especially if they have also felt the loneliness and fear that come with the loss of spiritual enthusiasm.

Fourth, during periods of dryness, small sins can become major handicaps. Often a petty vice or a small jealousy can be the stumbling block that prevents your forward movement. Take an especially critical look at your own

145

behavior. You may be clinging to some selfish act that is seriously interfering with your ability to be open to God. During hard times one must take seriously the New Testament call to repentance and change of life.

Finally, forms of prayer for these times of crisis must be simple. The one-minute exercises are particularly useful, especially the simplest forms, such as the repetition of a single word or phrase. Reading the Psalms may be helpful; certainly the psalmists understood the meaning of suffering. Your personal rule of life is especially critical during periods of aridity. Go over your written personal rule: You may find that you have slipped from regular observances and exercises. Work at following the rule, even if the exercise seems pointless. The discipline of prayer before automatic behaviors may well be the only thing that keeps one praying at all. New understandings are often the result of long and hard effort.

The following one-minute exercise is designed for times of spiritual dryness.

Exercise 3 in Persistence: One Minute of Resignation

Begin with a review of your present moment—not just of your physical surroundings, but of your thoughts and feelings as well. Where are you; what is happening in your mind? Allow your feelings to surface, especially the feelings of failure and frustration that often attend aridity. You may feel angry at God, or disappointed, or simply bored and tired by all the effort. Allow yourself awareness of whatever feelings you find. Then, without making any attempt to resolve them, place your feelings in the hands of God. Consciously, give everything over to Him. Do not try to establish a dialogue with God, do not try to reason things out, do not attempt to strike any bargains. Your inner monologue may sound like this:

"I'm tired and miserable and frustrated. This prayer stuff feels like a lot of garbage, just talking to myself. Here it is, God, misery and all. I'm turning this over to you."

Take whatever comes to mind—frustrations, disappointments, fears, doubts, resentments, angers—the whole ball of spiritual misery—and hand it over to God. Then repeat the words of Jesus, spoken from the cross:

"My God, my God, why have you forsaken me?"

Let these words settle in your mind for a few seconds, and then end the exercise with the final words of Jesus:

"Father, into your hands I commend my spirit."

Whatever the status of your spiritual life as you read this page, know that there will come a time when you find yourself at the dark end of the tunnel. Take a minute to do this exercise now, whether today is one of your peaks or one of your valleys.

Take a minute to practice resignation to God before reading on.

Job suffered, and complained to God. He demanded explanations for his pain, and reasons for human misery and suffering. God's answer was a question: Where were you when I made the world? God's answer is still the same. We complain that things are confusing and hurtful and that we simply do not understand why that is so. God's answer is still a question: How can you hope to understand? Our periods of dryness painfully remind us of our smallness before God. But, as Saint Paul has said, our

147

strength is made perfect in our weakness. We live with the promise of faith, the pledge of the Resurrection. We are assured that we have been redeemed, we have been bought back from our own failure, resignation, and despair. At our lowest times we are closest to God. In our depths He reaches out to us. It is only one step from the bottom of the dry well to the mountaintop. That step is God's; He will take it if you let Him.

14 · What's in It for Me?

"There is no free lunch." We all do things for reasons. We invest ourselves in an activity only with the expectation of some profit. There are many sorts of profit—material, physical, emotional, spiritual—and suggesting that people have reasons for what they do is not to say that all reasons are selfish or ignoble. Different activities are undertaken with different goals in mind, some of which are very positive. People occasionally give large sums of money to charity with no expectation of return on the funds invested. However, they may feel better about themselves for having made the contribution, and that good feeling is their just profit. It is a basic fact of human life that people will not continue any activity for very long without getting something out of it. This is as true of prayer as it is of anything else. If there is no reward for spiritual exercises, even brief forms of prayer will eventually be given up.

What can anybody get out of prayer and the practice of religion? This is an important question, and some answers frequently given seem almost to caricature biblical faith.

One common answer can be summarized as "pie in the sky by and by." Going to church and living by the commandments are said to earn passage through the pearly gates. Be moderately religious now, even though it may not mean that much or be very satisfying, and the payoff will be heaven. There is not much to lose, and lots to be gained—"someday." While we share the belief that the Christian is promised eternal life in the presence of God, too much focus on heaven-as-reward obscures a core element of Jesus' message: The Kingdom of God has already begun, and it is to be lived in the present life.

The Christian is immersed in this world, and this is as it should be. The "Word became flesh." He entered our world, our flesh, our lives. Christ is to be a part of daily living, not just an element in our daydreams of a happier future. We are to hope for heaven, but to live where we are. The goal of the brief spiritual exercise is to sanctify the present moment, to develop a sense of the holiness of everyday life—not to earn points for heaven.

Another response to the question seems to be gaining acceptance in American religion—faith and worship are thought to bring material benefits. Prosperity, health, and general well-being are promised to those accepting Jesus as their personal savior. Americans have long wanted to see material prosperity as a sign of God's blessing. We recently heard a television preacher tell his audience that it was God's will that they send him a donation right away. He told them to mark their calendars, showing the day that the check was mailed. They would, he assured them, experience an immediate increase in their incomes after sending the check. Unfortunately, that preacher is not an unusual case. There are others who tell us that if we will "pop the Jesus pill," we will get the next promotion, feel better about ourselves, and gain fulfillment of all our wishes. Certainly no more blatant sale of indulgences went on in the days before the Protestant Reformation.

Such solicitations are, to put it charitably, distortions of Christian faith. If they were true, only pagans and sinners would be poor, and poverty would be a sure sign of God's displeasure. Nothing could be further from the truth: In Jesus, God emptied Himself, taking on the form of a servant. Jesus lived with the poor, and warned the rich that their possessions might well be their undoing. Jesus promises us the cross, not fancy cars and freedom from material worries. The goal of prayer is a new sense of what is really important, not a more efficient scheme for satisfying the old material lusts.

The question remains: What is the payoff for prayer and spiritual development? If there is nothing to be gained, why even bother? The answer is found in Scripture and in traditional understandings the church has long maintained. Busy Christians cannot live their faith in the world by twisting it to meet the shallow expectations of a materialistic society. Neither can they live it by ignoring the demands of real life, postponing religious fulfillment to a future beyond the grave. We live out our religious commitment day-to-day. The payoff for a life of prayer comes as we learn that the present moment is the one that really counts, and that God cares about how this moment is lived.

A woman recounting her religious search told of reading Thomas Merton's autobiography, *The Seven Storey Mountain.* She was amazed, she said, to read of that moment when Merton walked by a church and felt strongly that God was calling out to him. "Imagine," she said, "really believing that there was somebody in there reaching out to you." That belief is the reward God gives for prayer.

God is trying to give us a message. He spoke to us in the Hebrew Scriptures, through Moses and the Prophets. He came to us in the person of Jesus. The message is clear: God loves us and cares about us, right here and right now. "Right here" for the Hebrews was a patch of desert, a mountain, and a tiny strip of land on the eastern end of the Mediterranean. Their "right now" was a relatively brief period ending nearly two thousand years ago. From that tiny place in that faraway time, God's message of love has gone forth to bless the world in all its places and all its times. God calls each of us to a never-ending moment of friendship with Him.

For I, Yahweh, your God,
I am holding you by the right hand;
I tell you, "Do not be afraid,
I will help you."
(Isaiah 41:13)

We are offered the opportunity to live in God's presence. His invitation is not a ticket to be cashed in at some time in the future, in heaven or when we get rich. He bids us to come into His presence now. This is the personal meaning of the wide sweep of God's designs. You are invited to become open to God in the present moment of life, wherever you happen to be. Merton felt called as he walked by a church, but he might have been on the subway instead. God is present in Chinese restaurants and on luxury liners and on buses full of illegal aliens being driven back across the border. Wherever one *is* is the best place to look for God. The Christian is called to experience God's grace in this very instant of time. No matter what one's past has held, no matter what the future may bring, the present moment is critical. We can share this moment with God.

Living in God's presence is not a pragmatic act. It will not get one to the front of the grocery store line any faster, though a minute of prayer offered then and there will remind one that the wait is shared with God. Living in God's presence will not fix all of life's hurts, but turning to the Scriptures may bring reassurance that God is there to help bear the pain. Living in God's presence will not bring more wealth, but God will enrich everything one has. The presence of God does not have practical utility.

Develop a personal rule of life and follow all of the suggestions given in this book, and the result may well be less free time, fewer chances to come out on top, more rejection from others, and more hours spent trying to figure out what God is trying to do with your life. Very little that God has to offer will make much difference at the bottom line of the world's ledger books. Perhaps we keep track of the wrong things. There is certainly a payoff for living in God's presence. That payoff goes by many names: Three of them are *peace, faith, and love.*

PEACE

With the presence of God comes "the peace of God which passes all understanding" (Philippians 4:7). This peace is like a deep pool at one's center. No matter what takes place at the surface or in the middle regions, the deep pool remains tranquil. The source of this peace is God Himself. As one grows closer to God, going beyond external observances, there comes a sense of His presence in all the twists and corners of life. God keeps cropping up from within one's own depths. That presence does not remove turmoil and uncertainty from life. Storms may rage on the surface and at deep levels within. Life may be filled with doubt, anxiety, physical and emotional suffering. Loved ones die, or become infirm. Careers turn sour. Money is lost. Relationships begin, develop, and end, sometimes painfully. The knowledge of God's presence is not a magic charm to ward off evil, doubt, and sadness. The peace of God at the center of the soul indeed passes all understanding. There is no discernible reason for it to be there at all—things can look dismal from the top of the pool. But living in the presence of God means that He is there in the dark moments as well as the bright ones. Life can be very hard indeed, yet God abides.

> Do not be afraid, for I have redeemed you;
> I have called you by your name, you are mine.
> Should you pass through the sea, I will be with you;
> or through rivers, they will not swallow you up.

Should you walk through fire, you will not be scorched
and the flames will not burn you.
For I am Yahweh, your God,
the holy one of Israel, your savior.
(Isaiah 43:1-3)

The peace which passes understanding does not alter
life's events. Rather, it radically shifts the context of those
events. The entire frame of reference changes. Because
God is seen at the heart of all reality, everything is understood in new ways. Happy moments are not just fleeting
pleasures, because they are seen to be an open sign of the
eternal goodness of God. Sad times become bearable, because they are shared with Jesus. At times God's peace
appears paradoxical: One is personally fulfilled because
personal fulfillment is no longer considered important.
This peace resists definition or description. But it is real,
and it is the result of a developed life of prayer. It comes
to those who remember that they live in the presence of
God.

FAITH

A deeper faith is another of the gifts flowing from life
lived in God's presence. In the original Greek, Scripture
calls faith the reality of things hoped for, the proof of
things not seen (Hebrews 11:1). This idea is much stronger
than the more usual understanding of faith as mental as-
sent to God's word in Scripture and the acceptance of
Christ as personal savior. A little boy came home from
Bible school, where they had been studying the Crucifixion. He was deeply worried about what was happening to
poor Jesus. "Don't worry," said his sage older brother, "it
all comes out fine in the end."

Faith is the knowledge—not the hope, but the knowledge—that our story also comes out fine in the end. By
faith we know that God is with us and that He will care
for our needs. Sometimes it seems impossible to hold that

assurance. Personal tragedy and global catastrophe bring doubt and despair. Only by faith can we penetrate the cloud of human suffering to experience God's design in what often seems to be a hopeless world. Live in God's presence and experience His peace. He will give one faith to move mountains.

LOVE

The richest payoff from living in the presence of God is an increased ability to love, and to accept love. It has been said that the truest fruit of prayer is deepening love. Love is another of those realities whose meaning is poorly conveyed and is finally diluted by words. Literature, art, and music have given love voice and tone and tint, and have not exhausted its depth. The Gospel tells us that God is love and that by remaining in love we remain in God and God remains in us. Through prayer, one comes to know that this is not just a cliché—it is literally true. Living in God's presence enhances all human love. Friendship, love between parents and children, married love— in fact all forms of love—are made new because He participates in our loving. Jesus gave love fresh meaning by his teaching and his example. As we strive to live always in his presence and by his example, our ability to love grows. His love and our love blend and become the same.

Prayer brings us Christ's gifts of peace and faith. These become active in us, and we reach beyond ourselves— this is Christ's love in action. Living with God present gives us direction in our lives as He leads us further into His life of loving service and concern. The prayerful Christian cannot be a passive observer of the world, because in Christ the work of prayer and the work of service are the same. If we accept the astounding premise that God loves us, we must also know that He loves our brothers and sisters as well. Once we know that God loves all men, women, and children, we can no longer deny the needs of others. Peace, faith, and love do not bring quiet contentment, pious self-satisfaction. Christian love brings us to action on behalf of humankind.

Acts growing out of Christian love are greatly needed in any time, and are especially critical in our own era. Life in our day is deeply disturbing. It is easy to insulate ourselves from the immense problems that surround us by yielding to a numbing sense of hopelessness. Our world cries out for exactly the opposite, and Christians must answer God's call to committed lives of services. Deeper spirituality of itself will not solve the problems of our time. However, the love of God, moving out through the loving service of prayerful people, gives hope to the world. Along with that hope comes a tremendous power to transform every corner of human life.

Jews and Christians have always been on the road, always been going somewhere. God brought Abraham from Haran to the land of Canaan. Moses was called to lead his people as they moved from slavery to the promised land. The people of Israel went into captivity and returned again. Jesus journeyed to Jerusalem, and his disciples were sent out and dispersed at Pentecost. Paul encountered Jesus on the road to Damascus, and then spent the rest of his life travelling as Christ's companion.

Each Christian life is a journey. Each moment is new, and the changes in life cannot be stopped, no matter how much we might want to stay where we are. There is no promise that the changes will all be comfortable or that every step of the journey will be filled with happiness and pleasure. But the final reward of prayer is that we need never travel alone: Jesus calls us to join him on the road. Others with whom we make the journey are also drawn into the divine companionship. Our travels with Jesus may take us across the planet or no farther than the edge of one's home town. The important variable is not the distance travelled, but the quality of the journey. One often moves farthest with God by standing absolutely still in His presence.

We travel a path of hope with Jesus, in the presence of God, and our lives proclaim to the world that God loves all the brothers and sisters in the human family. God is present with us now, and He waits for us at the end of life and at the end of history. He calls the entire human community to a future with Him. The New Testament closes at the place that is both the beginning and the end of the journey. Its final prayer—"Come, Lord Jesus" (Revelation 22:20)—calls us to step bravely toward that future, which already exists, right here, right now.

Bibliography

This is a list of books—some current and some centuries old—that we have found helpful and have often suggested to others. The editions noted are generally available in American bookstores and libraries.

Bonhoffer, Dietrich. *Life Together.* Translated by John Doberstein. New York: Harper and Row, 1954. Bonhoffer offers brief meditations on community, living with others, facing ourselves, ministry, confession, and communion.
———. *The Cost of Discipleship.* Translated by R. H. Fuller. New York: Macmillan, 1967. This is a magnificent treatise on costly grace and the call to discipleship, written by a twentieth-century martyr. Bonhoffer, killed by the Nazis in 1945, demonstrates to the reader that grace is free, but not cheap.
Capps, Walter, and Wendy Wright, eds. *Silent Fire: An Invitation to Western Mysticism.* San Francisco: Harper and Row, 1978. This anthology of readings from the great authors in Christian mysticism spans the centuries from the earliest writers to contemporary sources.
The Cloud of Unknowing. Garden City: Image Books, 1973. This is a fourteenth-century masterwork on the Christian mystical experience. The unknown English author speaks to our contemporary world of knowing God in the face of His apparent absence in a "cloud of unknowing." It is a very practical and down-to-earth book of tremendous power and literary style.

Foster, Richard J. *Celebration of Discipline.* San Francisco: Harper and Row, 1978. In this very current book, Foster shows the contemporary importance of such ancient spiritual disciplines as fasting, simplicity, service, and confession.

Holmes, Urban. *Turning to Christ.* New York: Seabury Press, 1981. Holmes presents a contemporary theology of renewal and evangelization, drawn from deep biblical roots, and develops authentic strategies for modern evangelists.

Ignatius of Loyola. *The Spiritual Exercises (A Literal Translation and a Contemporary Reading).* Translated by David J. Fleming. St. Louis: Institute of Jesuit Sources, 1978. This is a spiritual classic from the sixteenth-century founder of the Jesuit order. The techniques for use of the imagination and emotions in prayer outlined by Ignatius are widely followed even today.

John of The Cross, Saint. *The Ascent of Mount Carmel.* Translated by E. Allison Peers. Garden City, N.Y.: Doubleday, 1958. This sixteenth-century priest wrote what many consider to be the definitive charting of the course of the soul's ascent to God through the stages of prayer.

———. *The Dark Night of the Soul.* Translated by E. Allison Peers. Garden City, N.Y.: Doubleday, 1959. This is a penetrating and always up-to-date analysis of what occurs when one seems to lose contact with God just as union seems imminent. The "Dark Night" precedes the dawning of the deepest stages of prayer.

Kelsey, Morton. *Encounter With God.* Minneapolis: Bethany Fellowship Inc., 1972. This is an excellent beginning book in Christian spirituality for those with some understanding of modern psychology, science, and philosophy. Kelsey explores the contemporary intellectual world and finds God in its avenues.

———. *The Other Side of Silence: A Guide to Christian Meditation.* New York: Paulist Press, 1976. This is a guide for the serious pursuit of meditation. Kelsey emphasizes silence and suggests uses for the imagination in this book for beginners as well as advanced meditators.

Kempis, Thomas à. *The Imitation of Christ.* Translated by Harold Gardiner. Garden City, N.Y.: Doubleday, 1955. This simple book on prayer is one of the most influential works in Christian history. It has been said that more Christians have read this book than have read any other except the Bible.

Lawrence of the Resurrection, Brother. *The Practice of the Presence of God.* New York: Doubleday, 1977. Brother Lawrence was a monastery cook who found that spiritual prayer grows out of the ordinary work of life. This is a simply written, but immensely helpful, book.

Leckey, Dolores. *The Ordinary Way: A Family Spirituality.* New York: Crossroads, 1982. Leckey makes specific and wise connections between monasticism and family life, and in this very innovative book presents a model for regular and ordered spirituality in the family context.

Leech, Kenneth. *True Prayer: An Invitation to Christian Spirituality.* San Francisco: Harper and Row, 1980. Leech, a pastor, theologian, and spiritual guide in the Church of England, makes a practical yet theologically sound presentation on prayer and the spiritual life for the educated Christian.

Maloney, George A. *Inward Stillness.* Denville, N.J.: Dimension Books, 1976. Maloney, a Western Jesuit, explores the riches of Eastern Christian spirituality and shows that hectic modern life can benefit greatly from the spiritual traditions of the East.

Marty, Martin. *A Cry of Absence.* San Francisco: Harper and Row, 1983. Easy to read, profound, and very moving, this book is for all those who experience the wintery times of the spiritual life. Marty makes a magnificent treatment of God's apparent absence in contemporary life.

Merton, Thomas. *Conjectures of a Guilty Bystander.* Garden City, N.Y. Image Books, 1959. Merton is perhaps the most significant Catholic spiritual writer of our century. This book deals with the great modern problems of war, injustice, and racial prejudice in the light of Christian spirituality.

———. *New Seeds of Contemplation.* New York: New Directions Books, 1961. This is a contemporary classic on contemplative prayer and its place in the modern world. Written for a monastic audience, it also speaks clearly to those of us who are not monks.

———. *Contemplative Prayer.* Garden City, N.Y.: Image Books, 1971. Merton writes here to a wider audience of Christian laity.

Nouwen, Henri. *The Way of The Heart*. New York: Seabury Press, 1981. Nouwen explores the spirituality of the desert fathers and demonstrates that their thinking still has much to offer us in the twentieth century.

———. *The Genesee Diary*. Garden City, N.Y.: Doubleday, 1981. This is Nouwen's diary of a seven-month stay as a member of a contemplative religious community. He shows that retreat from the world can also deepen involvement in the active life.

Pennington, M. Basil. *Centering Prayer*. Garden City, N.Y. Doubleday, 1982. Pennington rediscovers and reinterprets the Jesus Prayer, one of the simplest and most effective forms of prayer ever devised.

Quoist, Michel. *Prayers*. New York: Avon, 1975. Widely acclaimed, usable by almost anyone, this is a popular and readable collection of prayers for our time.

Teresa of Avila. *The Interior Castle*. Translated by E. Allison Peers. Garden City, N.Y.: Doubleday, 1961. One of history's most remarkable women has left us her description of the journey to God. Her work remains as relevant today as it was when written in the sixteenth century.

Underhill, Evelyn. *Mysticism*. New York: E. P. Dutton, 1961. This English laywoman was considered one of the leading spiritual directors of her time. She offers practical advice from a profound understanding of scripture, history, and theology.

Ward, Bendicta. *The Sayings of the Desert Fathers*. London: Mowbray, 1975. This is an encyclopedic collection of the sayings of these early Christian monks and nuns. The close ties between the traditional spirituality of East and West are readily visible to the thoughtful reader.

About the Authors

Christopher Carstens, Ph.D.
Christopher Carstens is a clinical psychologist specializing in the treatment of children and adolescents. He received his doctorate from the University of Connecticut and has published several papers on behavioral therapy and treatment. He is also a frequent speaker at professional conferences and workshops.

Dr. Carstens lives in San Diego with his wife and two children and is an active community leader.

William P. Mahedy
William P. Mahedy is an Episcopal priest who served as a U.S. Army Chaplain with one tour in Vietnam. Under the auspices of the Veterans Administration, he co-authored the design for the Vietnam Veterans Outreach Program. He has also written and lectured extensively on the psychological, moral and religious impact of the Vietnam war on its veterans as well as on ethical and moral issues arising from nuclear war.

Fr. Mahedy lives in San Diego with his wife and two children and is currently Episcopal Campus Pastor at the University of California at San Diego and San Diego State University.